A Brief Dictionary of Economic Terms

3rd Edition
Expanded and illustrated

Edited by
Edward Robert Raupp
and
Danna Vance Raupp

Great Bay Community College
Portsmouth, New Hampshire

Blue Impala Press
2016

A BRIEF DICTIONARY OF ECONOMIC TERMS,
3rd Edition

The typeface for the text is 12-point Garamond.

Published by Blue Impala Press
10 Hillside Road
North Hampton, NH 03862

ISBN-13: 978-1535043168
ISBN-10: 1535043164

For our students, wherever they may be

Introduction

In a sense, every university class is a foreign language class. Economics fits that model. There are strange words, like "oligopsony," and words that are familiar but have different meanings to economists, like "elasticity." This book aims to help students to make sense of the vocabulary of economics.

No claim is made to originality. The definitions in this book have their origins in many works, and some of these are listed in the References section. And no effort was made to identify each definition with its source, since many are mixtures and some are seasoned with our own comments.

When I was first invited to teach economics in the United States, I asked a student how she liked the course she had just completed—it happened to be the same macroeconomics course I was about to start teaching. She said, "It was boring and irrelevant to my life!" From that moment, I pledged to myself and to my students that I would make every effort to ensure that such a comment would never come from any of my students. One of my approaches has been to define economics terms in ways that students could understand and that were relevant to their lives; I hope this little book helps.

The first edition of this book was prepared for Gori University students in the former Soviet Republic of Georgia. Any revenues above the cost of printing will go to the English Library at Gori University. Why a third edition? Students, lecturers, and others have requested it, and the language of business and economics continues to evolve. Events of the past few years have given rise to new language, some of which seems almost unintelligible. Some of this language is included in this updated edition.

—ERR

❧ A ❧

AAA—Triple A rating, the highest bond rating of Standard & Poor, which rates financial securities on the basis of their risk.

ability to pay—The principle that any tax should fall on those who can best afford to pay.

absolute advantage—Occurs when a country's workers are more productive at producing a good than another country's workers. (Contrast with *comparative advantage.*)

accident insurance—A type of health insurance coverage that only provides benefits for an insured's death, dismemberment, disability, or medical care that results from the insured being in an accident.

account—The basic tool that a company uses to record, group, and summarize similar types of financial transactions.

accounting—A system or set of rules and methods for collecting, recording, summarizing, reporting, and analyzing a company's financial information.

accounting profit—Definition of profit used by accountants that states profit is total revenue minus explicit measurable costs. (Contrast with *economic profit.*)

accounts payable—The money that a firm owes to its suppliers. A liability account that represents a contractual promise of payment by the holder of the account to another party.

accounts receivable—The money owed to a firm by its customers. An asset account that represents a contractual promise by another party to pay an amount to the holder of the account.

accrual-basis accounting—An accounting system in which a company records revenues when they are earned and expenses when they are incurred, even if the company has not yet received the revenues or paid the expenses.

accrued income—(1) In accounting, income that has already been earned, but which is not receivable until a specified date in the next accounting period. (2) In investments, the amount of interest that has been earned on a bond, but which is not yet payable to the bondholder as of the financial reporting date.

acquisition—A company buys another company and controls the resulting venture but does not necessarily exercise direct control. (See *takeover*.)

acquisition expenses—Costs that are directly attributable to the production of new business.

active financial management strategy—An investment strategy in which an asset manager views any security in a portfolio as potentially tradable, if doing so would improve the portfolio's performance.

activists—Those who consider the private sector to be relatively unstable and able to absorb economic shocks only with the aid of some government intervention.

actuarial assumptions—The estimated values [for such elements of insurance product design as mortality rates, investment earnings, expenses, and policy lapses] on which an insurer bases its product pricing and policy reserve calculations.

actuary—A technical expert in insurance, annuities, and financial instruments who applies mathematical knowledge to industry and company statistics to calculate an insurance company's mortality rates, morbidity rates, lapse rates, premium rates, policy reserves, and other financial values.

adaptive expectations—A theory of how people form their views about the future that assumes they do so using past trends and the errors in their own earlier predictions. Contrast with rational expectations.

adjusting entry—An accounting entry that a company makes to record internal financial transactions or correct errors that occur in one or more accounting periods.

advanced developing countries—A term for those less developed countries (LDCs) with particularly rapid industrial development.

advanced economies—A term used by the International Monetary Fund (IMF) for the top group in its hierarchy of advanced economies, countries in transition, and developing countries.

adverse selection—The tendency for unobserved attributes to become undesirable from the standpoint of an uninformed party.

after-tax dollars. Money that has been taxed.

Age Discrimination in Employment Act (ADEA)—A United States federal law that protects workers age 40 and older from being discriminated against because of their age.

agency—A legal relationship in which one party, known as the principal, authorizes another party, known as the agent, to act on the principal's behalf.

agent—One who performs an act for another person, the principal.

aggregate demand—Total demand for goods and services in the economy. The total quantity of all goods and services that people are willing to buy at different price levels.

aggregate expenditures—Total planned spending on goods and services in the economy.

aggregate income—The sum of all income earned by resource suppliers in an economy during a given time period.

aggregate output—The total quantity of final goods and services produced in an economy during a given time period.

aggregate supply—Total production of goods and services in the economy. The total quantity of all goods and services produced at different price levels.

aggressive financial strategy—A financial management strategy that places an unusually strong emphasis on profitability and de-emphasizes solvency.

agribusiness—A term that reflects the large, corporate nature of many farm enterprises in the modern economy.

agricultural economics—A specialization in microeconomics that deals with production and distribution of food and fiber.

agrifirms—Large firms that own huge farms and operate them like big corporations.

alien corporation—From the point of view of any nation or any state in the United States, a company that is incorporated under the laws of another state or country. Contrast with *domestic corporation*.

alternative goods—Other goods that use some of the same type of resources used to produce the good in question.

American Stock Exchange—Former name of NYSE Amex Equities, a key stock exchange in the United States. It consists mainly of stocks and bonds of companies that are small to medium-sized, compared with shares of large corporations traded on the New York Stock Exchange.

NYSE Euronext acquired the American Stock Exchange on October 1, 2008.

Americans with Disabilities Act (ADA)—A U.S. federal law that protects individuals with disabilities against all types of discrimination, including employment discrimination.

amortized cost—An asset's historical cost, less any adjustment, such as depreciation or amortization, to the asset's book value.

annual percentage rate (APR)—The cost of credit calculated as an annual percentage.

annual report—Report to stockholders containing a summary of the year's operations and pertinent financial information.

annuity—(1) A series of periodic payments. (2) A financial contract between an insurer and a customer under which the insurer promises to make a series of periodic benefit payments to a named individual—the payee—in exchange for the contract owner's payment of a premium or series of premiums to the insurer.

antiselection—The tendency of individuals who suspect or know they are more likely than average to experience loss to apply for or renew insurance to a greater extent than people who lack such knowledge of probable loss. Also known as adverse selection and selection against the company.

antitrust judgment by performance—View that competitiveness of markets should be judged by the behavior of firms in that market, not by the size of firms or the structure of the market.

antitrust judgment by structure—View that competitiveness of markets should be judged by the structure of the industry. A more highly concentrated industry is less competitive than one that is less highly concentrated.

antitrust law—A policy or action that seeks to promote competition by curtailing monopolistic powers and restraint of trade within a market.

antitrust policy—Government's policy toward the competitive process, intended to improve competitiveness of markets.

a posteriori—After the fact. Relating to or derived by reasoning from observed facts. Findings about a proposition after investigation.

a priori—From first principles. Assumptions of *a priori* arguments are axioms that cannot be derived from empirical evidence.

APEC—Asia-Pacific Economic Cooperation.

appreciation—A rise in the value of an asset and the opposite of depreciation. When the value of a currency rises relative to another, it appreciates. Contrast with *depreciation*.

arbitrage—Buying in one market where price is low and selling in another market simultaneously where the price is higher.

arc elasticity—The average elasticity or a range of points on a demand curve.

articles of incorporation—The document that organizers of a
company seeking incorporation must file with a state
agency. The document contains the essential features of a
proposed company, including its name, the location of its
principal place of business, the kind of business it will
transact, and the names of its original directors.

ASEAN—Association of Southeast Asian Nations.

Asian tigers—Asian nations having achieved so much economic
growth they are no longer considered developing countries:
Taiwan, South Korea, Singapore, and Hong Kong.

The Republic of Korea has risen from the ashes of war to become an "Asian Tiger."

assembly line—A manufacturing system in which products are
assembled by moving them from one worker or machine to
another. Application of principle of specialization and
division of labor noted by Adam Smith in *Wealth of Nations*.

asset—A possession of value, usually measured in terms of
money. An item of value owned by an individual or a
company. Examples of assets include cash, computer
equipment, investments, buildings, furniture, and land.

asset demand for money—Money demanded as a store of value.

assumptions—Beliefs or statements presupposed to be true.

asymmetric information—An inequality in the information
known by each party to a transaction. A perfectly
competitive market assumes symmetry.

audit—The process of examining and evaluating a company's records and procedures to ensure that accounting records and financial statements are accurate and reliable, the company maintains quality assurance, and operational procedures and policies are effective and legally compliant.

auditor's opinion—A statement, prepared by an independent public accounting company, that attests that the information contained in a company's annual report fairly represents the operations of the company and that the audit was conducted in accordance with generally accepted auditing standards (GAAS).

audit trail—A chronological, sequential set of accounting records and reports from the beginning to the end of a business transaction.

Austrian economists—Economists who believed economics should be a purely deductive, but nonmathematical study. Friedrich Hayek, Viennese economist, was one of its most notable proponents, embracing an extremist philosophy of pure libertarianism with no involvement by the government, an approach contributing to the Great Depression.

autarky—A situation of national self-sufficiency in which there is no economic interaction with foreigners.

automatic stabilizers—Features of the economic system that reduce the impact of the business cycle. They put money into the economy during periods of recession and take money out during periods of inflation. Examples: unemployment compensation, needs based financial aid, and graduated progressive income tax system.

automobile insurance—A type of insurance that protects an insured from financial losses arising from the operation of a vehicle.

autonomous consumption—That part of consumption which
   does not depend on current income.

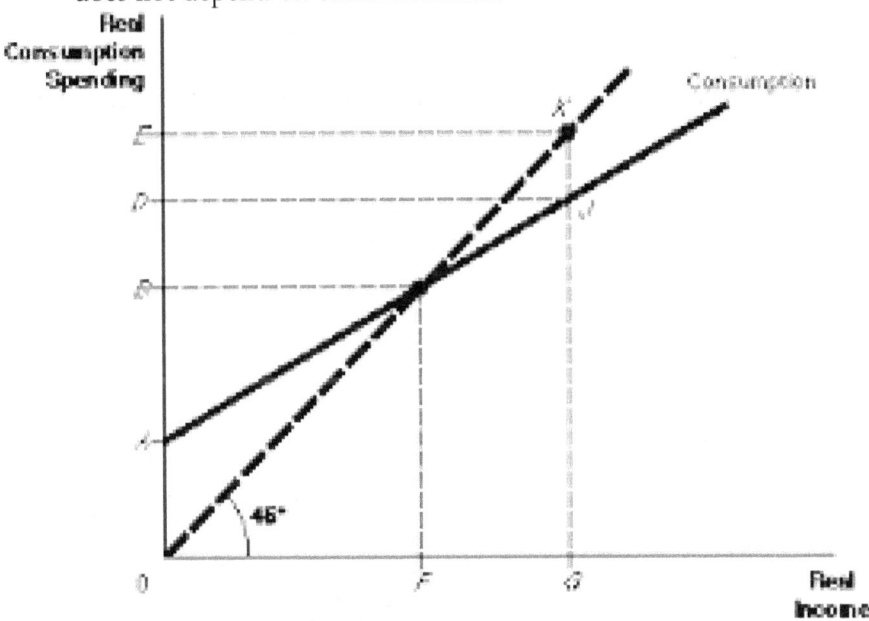

There is consumption even when there is no income.
Consumers draw on savings and borrow in order to consume.

autonomous government purchases—Government spending that
   does not vary with the level of real GDP.
average—A number expressing the central or typical value in a
   set of data, in particular the mode, median, or (most
   commonly) the mean, which is calculated by dividing the
   sum of the values in the set by their number.
average cost—Total cost (TC) divided by the amount produced.
   (See *average total cost.*)
average fixed cost (AFC)—Equals total fixed costs / total
   product

average product (AP)—Total output divided by the quantity of the variable input.

average revenue (AR)—Total revenue divided by the amount produced.

average tax rate (or ratio)—The percentage of overall income that is paid in taxes.

average total cost (ATC)—Equals total cost / total product.

average total cost in the short and long runs—Because fixed costs are variable in the long run, ATC in the short run differs from that in the long run.

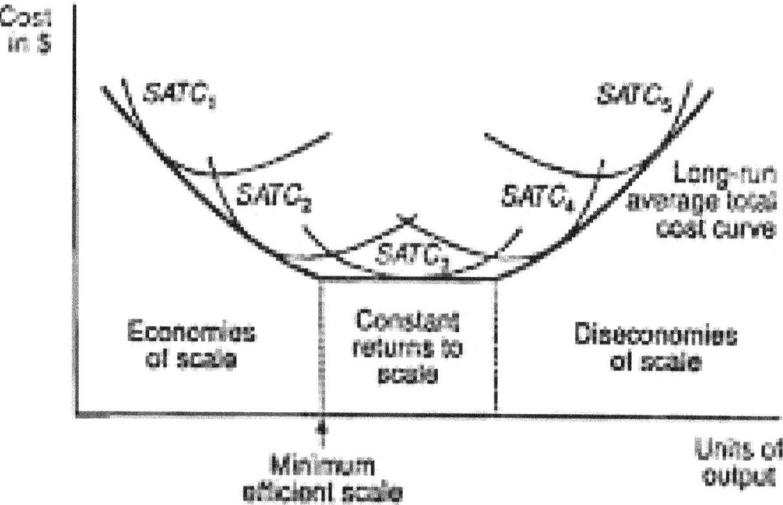

Short-run ATCs nest in an envelope formed by ATC in the long run.

average variable cost (AVC)—Equals total variable cost / total product.

axiom—A self-evident proposition, i.e., one that is believed to be true, but must be assumed and cannot be proved.

❧ B ❧

backwardation—When a commodity is valued more highly in a spot market (that is, when it is for delivery today) than in a futures market (for delivery at some point in the future).

bailout—A capital infusion offered to a business with a national or multi-national footprint that is in danger of bankruptcy, insolvency, or liquidation. Financial aid can be provided in the form of debt or equity offerings, cash contributions, or a form of loan or line of credit, and often accompanied by greater government oversight and regulation. The failure of a business that employs thousands or plays an influential role in the economy can send shock waves throughout the economy, including other industries. The credit crisis that began in 2007 created numerous failures around the world, which resulted in a large number of government-sponsored bailouts in almost every industry across the globe.

balance of payments—A country's record of all transactions between its residents and the residents of all other nations. A summary of the flow if international transactions. An accounting statement of the money value of international transactions between one nation and the rest of the world over a specific period of time. The statement shows the sum of transactions of individuals, businesses, and government agencies located in one nation, against those of all other nations.

balance of trade—The difference between the value of the goods a nation exports and the value of the goods it imports. That part of a nation's balance of payments dealing with imports and exports—i.e., trade in goods and services—over a given period. If the money value of exports exceeds that of imports, the trade balance is said to be "favorable"; if the money value of imports exceeds that of exports, the trade balance is said to be "unfavorable."

balance sheet—A financial statement that shows a company's financial condition or position as of a specified date; summarizes what a company owns (assets), what it owes (liabilities), and its owners' investment in the company (owners' equity) on a specified date. Also known as statement of financial position.

balanced budget multiplier—An increase in government purchases by $1 funded by an equal increase in household taxes will cause GDP to increase by $1.

balanced budget amendment—Proposed amendment to the U.S. Constitution requiring a balanced federal budget. No rational person, and certainly no reputable economist, supports this simplistic approach to budgeting.

balanced growth—Growth of all sectors of an economy at the same proportional rate.

balanced growth plan—Spreading development money simultaneously among all sectors of a country's economy.

bank—A financial institution whose main functions are taking in deposits and lending funds to borrowers.

Bank of England—The central bank of the United Kingdom.

barrier to entry—Social, political, legal, or economic impediment that prevents firms from entering a market. Example: One firm owns a patent on a product, so other firms are legally barred from entering the market for that product.

barrier to exit—Social, political, legal, or economic impediment that prevents firms from leaving that market. Example: A firm builds a plant in a country whose laws bar businesses from leaving the country.

barter—An exchange of goods and services without money.

base year—The reference year, with a value of 100, used in the construction of index numbers.

basis point (bp)—An increment of 0.01 percent; e.g., half a percent is equal to 50 bp, and one and a half percent is equal to 150 bp.

bear—An investor who thinks that the price of a particular security or class of securities is going to fall; the opposite of a bull.

bear market—A market in which, in a time of falling prices, shareholders may rush to sell their stock shares, adding to the downward momentum.

before-tax dollars. Money that has not been taxed.

beggar-thy-neighbor—A policy that seeks advantage for the residents of one country at the expense of another.

behavioral economics—The subfield of economics that integrates the insights of psychology.

benchmarking—The process by which a company compares its own performance, products, and services with those of other organizations that are recognized as the best in a particular category. The product or service that is determined to be the industry standard is known as a benchmark.

benefits-received principle—The belief that taxes should be paid by those who benefit from a government program or service.

Benelux Union—Formerly Benelux Economic Union. Aims at closer economic and legal cooperation and integration between Belgium, Netherlands, and Luxembourg.

beta coefficient—A measure of the volatility of a stock price. Beta measures the sensitivity of the price of a particular asset to changes in the market as a whole. If a company's shares have a beta of 0.8, it implies that on average the share price will change by 0.8% if there is a 1% change in the market.

Beveridge curve—a graph of the relationship between
   unemployment and the job vacancy rate (the number of
   unfilled jobs expressed as a proportion of the labor force).

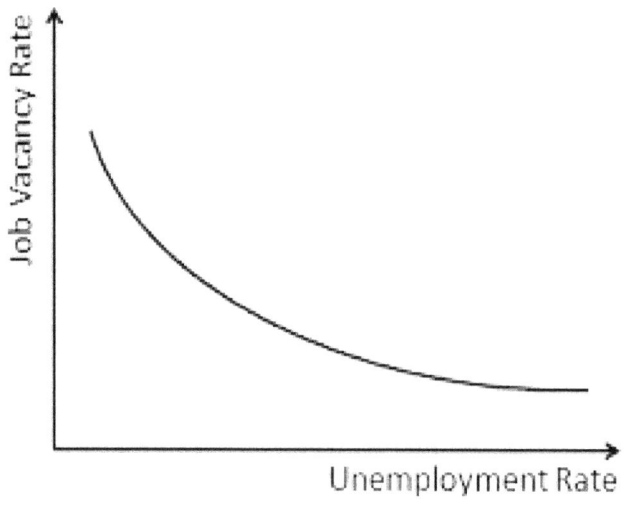

Beveridge curve

big data—Extremely large data sets that may be analyzed
   computationally to reveal patterns, trends, and associations,
   especially relating to human behavior and interactions.
Big Mac index—Calculation based on the theory of purchasing-
   power parity, the notion that a dollar should buy the same
   amount in all countries. In the long run, the exchange rate
   between two countries should move towards the rate that
   equalizes the price of an identical basket of goods and
   services in each country. One "basket" is a McDonald's Big
   Mac, which is produced in about 120 countries. The Big
   Mac PPP is the exchange rate that would mean hamburgers
   cost the same in America as abroad. Comparing actual
   exchange rates with PPPs indicates whether a currency is
   under- or over-valued.

bilateral monopoly—A market in which there is only a single
    seller and a single buyer.

black market—Trading that violates laws restricting free markets.
    An illegal market in which goods are sold above their legal
    price.

Black Sea Economic Cooperation Zone (BSEC)—Aims to
    enhance regional stability through economic cooperation.
    Members include Albania, Armenia, Azerbaijan, Bulgaria,
    Georgia, Greece, Moldova, Romania, Russia, Turkey, and
    Ukraine

black swan theory—A metaphor that encapsulates the concept
    that the event is a surprise (to the observer) and has a major
    impact. After the fact, the event is rationalized by hindsight.
    Developed by Nassim Nicholas Taleb. Taleb regards almost
    all major scientific discoveries, historical events, and artistic
    accomplishments as "black swans"—undirected and
    unpredicted. He gives the rise of the Internet, the personal
    computer, World War I, and the September 11 attacks as
    examples of Black Swan Events.

A black swan, a member of the species Cygnus atratus,
which remained undocumented in the West until the eighteenth century

blue chip—Shares of the largest and most prestigious corporations.

bond—A debt security whereby the bond issuer promises to pay the bondholder a stated rate of interest over a specified period of time, at the end of which time, the original amount of borrowed money must be repaid. The owner of the bond is known as the bondholder. The entity that sells the bond to raise money is known as the bond issuer.

bond principal—The sum the issuer of a bond borrows from the bond's initial purchaser. This amount, which is stated on the face of the bond, is payable by the issuer of the bond on or before the bond's maturity date. Also known as bond's face value, maturity value, and par value.

bond rating—A letter grade assigned by a bond rating agency that indicates the credit quality of a bond issue. (AAA is the highest rating given by Standard & Poor.)

bond-rating agency—A firm that evaluates the creditworthiness of governments and corporations that issues bonds. Standard & Poor and Moody's are the two leading U.S. bond-rating agencies.

book value—The value that is placed on the net assets of a firm.

borrower—An individual who has received and used something belonging to someone else, with the intention of returning or repaying it, often with interest in the case of borrowed money.

bottom-up budgeting—A budget-setting approach for business organizations that requires lower-level managers to prepare their own departmental budgets for approval by upper-level managers.

bounded rationality—The argument that there is a finite limit to the amount of information the human brain can hold.

boycott—An agreement among individuals or competing
    companies to refrain from doing business with another
    company.
brain drain—The outflow of the best and brightest students from
    developing countries to developed countries.
break-even point—The level of output at which income from
    sales just equals fixed and variable costs.

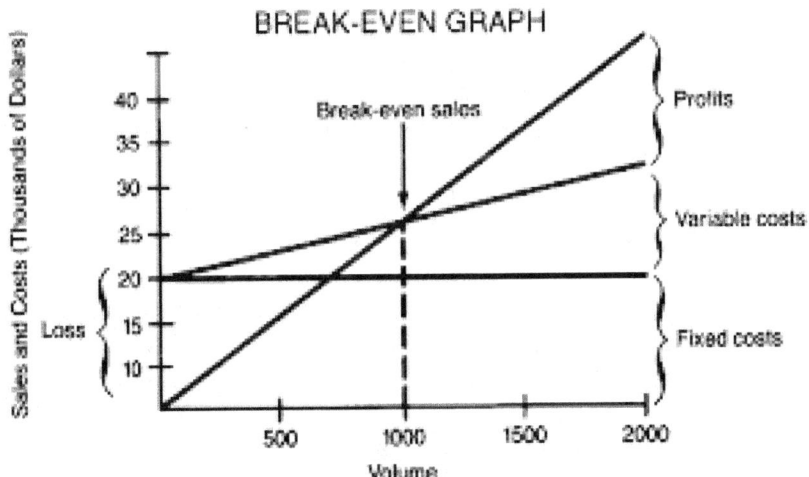

BREAK-EVEN GRAPH

Bretton Woods system—An 1944 agreement reached in Bretton
    Woods, New Hampshire, that governed international
    financial relationships from the period after World War II
    until 1971. Two principal organizations of the system are
    the International Monetary Fund (IMF) and the
    International Bank for Reconstruction and Development
    (IBRD, better known as the World Bank).
BREXIT—A movement by proponents in Britain to leave the
    European Union (EU). In a referendum on June 23, 2016,
    the majority of voters opted to leave the EU.

BRICS nations—A group of emerging countries with 3 billion people, 42 percent of the world's population, thought to have potential for rapid growth: Brazil, Russia, India, China, and South Africa. Recently, Brazil and Russia have encountered severe economic setbacks, partly due to falling oil prices, partly due to wide-spread corruption.

broad money—A general term for M2.

bubble—When the price of an asset rises far higher than can be explained by fundamentals, such as the income likely to derive from holding the asset.

budget—A financial plan of action, expressed in monetary terms, which covers income and spending a specified time period, such as one year.

budget constraint—A graph showing the maximum affordable combinations of two goods for a household when spending all of the household's disposable income.

budget deficit—The amount each year by which government spending is greater than its income.

budget surplus—The amount each year by which government income is greater than its spending.

bull—An investor who expects the price of a particular security to rise; the opposite of a bear.

bull market—A market in which there is a continuous rise in stock prices.

bundling—A pricing strategy in which the firm sells two or more products together at a single price.

Bureau of Economic Analysis—An agency in the U.S. Department of Commerce that provides official macroeconomic and industry statistics including the gross domestic product of the United States.

business—A private producing unit in our society.

business confidence—How the people who run companies feel about their organizations' prospects.

business cycle—Fluctuations in business activity: expansion,
  peak, downturn, and trough.

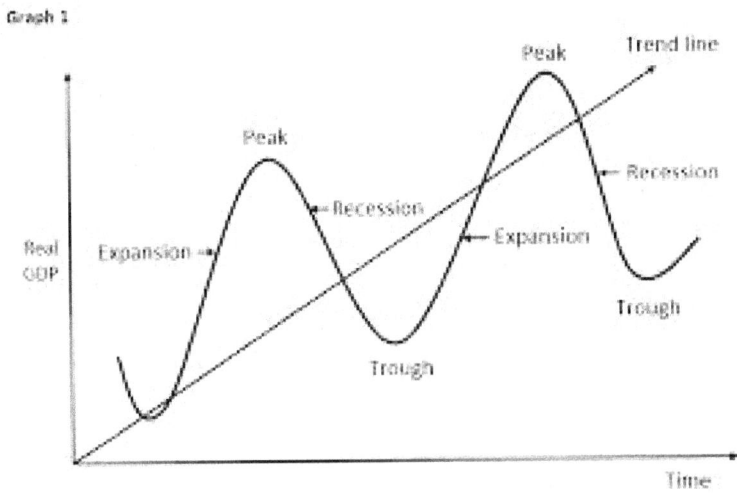

Business cycle

business cycle theory—The study of macroeconomic
  fluctuations. Mainstream theory is that potential GDP
  grows at a steady rate while aggregate demand grows at a
  fluctuating rate.
business economics—An area of economic study and application
  concerned with the analysis of the behavior of firms in
  markets and industries and with the determination of costs
  and prices.
business plan—A description of an enterprise including its name,
  goals and objectives, the product(s) sold and distributed,
  the work skills needed to produce those products, and the
  marketing strategies used to promote them.
buyer's market—A market in which supply seems plentiful and
  prices seem low; the opposite of a seller's market.

capacity—The maximum number of units a firm can produce. Also the maximum output of a nation.

capital—The physical equipment (buildings, machines, vehicles, etc.) and human labor and skills used in the production of goods and services. Capital consists of all goods produced by human labor (with other resources) and used in the production of still more goods and services; in other words, produced means of production. Some examples are machinery, houses and other buildings, grapevines, fruit trees and hogs on the hoof, education, training, and health care. Also used to refer to corporate equity, debt securities, and cash.

capital account—The part of the balance of payments account that lists all long-term flows of payments.

capital adequacy ratio—The ratio of a bank's capital to its total assets, required by regulators to be above a minimum ("adequate") level so there is little risk of the bank going bankrupt.

capital budget—A budget that shows a company's plans for the financial management of its long-term, high-cost investment proposals, such as new investments, major repairs to or remodeling of existing investments, acquisitions of other companies or lines of business, mandated safety and environmental improvements, expense reduction projects, and revenue expansion projects.

capital controls—A government's prohibitions on its currency freely flowing into and out of the country.

capital flight—When capital flows rapidly out of a country, usually because something happens which causes investors suddenly to lose confidence in its economy. (See *Raupp's rule of capital flow.*)

capital gain—Increase in the value of one's assets in a specified period of time. The amount by which the selling price of an asset exceeds its purchase price. Contrast with capital loss.

capital intensive—A production process that involves large amounts of capital; the opposite of *labor intensive*.

capital-labor tradeoff—Analysis of the effect of substituting capital for labor and vice versa.

capitalism—An economic and political system in which a country's trade and industry are controlled by private owners for profit, rather than by the state. Another term for market economy or free enterprise system. An economic system in which the means of production are privately owned and controlled and which is characterized by competition, the profit motive, and consumer choice. Efficiency is emphasized often at the expense of equity. There are no purely capitalist economies in the world. (Contrast with *socialism* and *mixed economy*.)

capitalists—Business people who have acquired large amounts of money and use it to invest in businesses.

capital loss—The amount by which the purchase price of an asset exceeds its selling price. Contrast with capital gain.

capital market—The market in which corporate equity and longer-term debt securities (those maturing in more than one year) are traded.

capital structure—The composition of a company's mixture of debt and equity financing. A firm's debt-equity ratio is often referred to as its *gearing*. Taking on more debt is known as gearing up, or increasing leverage.

cartel—A group of firms (or nations) that colludes, jointly setting price and output. A combination of firms that acts like a single firm. OPEC is a cartel of oil producing nations.

cartel model of oligopoly—Model that assumes that oligopolies act as if they were a single monopoly.

cash-basis accounting—An accounting system in which a company recognizes revenues or expenses only when it receives or disburses cash.

cash budget—A type of budget that projects a company's beginning cash balance, cash inflows, cash outflows, and ending cash balance for a specified accounting period, typically by quarter.

cash flow—Money coming into and going out of a firm. A cash inflow is a source of funds and a cash outflow is a use of funds.

cash flow statement—A financial statement that provides information about an insurer's cash receipts (inflows) and its cash disbursements (outflows) during a specified period.

catch-up effect—In any period, the economies of countries that start off poor generally grow faster than the economies of countries that start off rich. (See *convergence*.)

causation—Term in statistics meaning that a change in one data point causes another data point to change.

central bank—A country's principal monetary authority, responsible for such key functions as issuing currency and regulating the supply of credit in the economy.

centrally planned economy—An economy in which a central planning board decides what, how, by whom products are supplied and consumed, e.g., USSR, North Korea, Cuba.

certificate of deposit (CD)—A contractual agreement issued by a bank that returns the investor's principal with interest on a specified date.

certificate of incorporation—A document issued by a state that grants a corporation its legal existence and right to operate as a corporation. Also known as corporate charter.

ceteris paribus—Latin, meaning "all else remaining constant." Holding all variables constant except for one.

change in demand—A shift in a given demand curve caused by one of the determinants of demand for the good, e.g., income, taste, or a change in the price of a substitute good.

change in quantity demanded—Movement along the demand curve for a good in response to a change in the price of the good.

change in quantity supplied—Movement along the supply curve for a good in response to a change in the price of the good.

change in supply—A shift in a given supply curve caused by one of the determinants of supply for the good, e.g., change in the price of one or more of the good's factors of production. Two of the more common changes are labor and energy.

character—In the context of credit transactions, character is one of the Three Cs of Credit (Character, Capital, and Capacity). It is an indicator of how creditworthy a prospective borrower is likely to be, as determined by the borrower's handling of past debts and stability in jobs and residences.

characteristics of money—Include being durable (both physically and socially), divisible (money can be divided into increments appropriate for the cost of an item), transportable (literally meaning that money must be easy to move), and the ability to regulate the amount of money in a market by making it uncounterfeitable.

charge account—An agreement between a consumer and a firm that enables the consumer to make purchases up to a specified limit without paying cash. Consumers then pay at a later time.

chargeback—A method for allocating costs within an organization that allocates indirect costs to departments based on a department's usage.

charter—A document issued by a state government granting a corporation permission to operate.

checking account—A bank account that allows a depositor to write checks.

checks—Written orders directing a bank to pay a person or organization a specific amount of money.

Chicago School—A free-market economic philosophy long associated with the University of Chicago.

choice—Decision made or course of action taken when faced with a set of alternatives.

churning—Unethical and often illegal sales practice designed to increase commission sales. (1) In insurance sales, churning can occur when an agent induces a policy owner to cash in a policy and buy another, even though the replacement is not in the policy owner's best interest. 2) In stock and bond sales, churning can occur when a broker engages in excessive and unwarranted trading of clients' accounts.

circular flow—The movement of output and income from one sector of the economy to another; often illustrated as a circular flow diagram.

Civil Rights Act of 1964—A U.S. federal anti-discrimination law that applies to employers that are engaged in interstate commerce and that have 15 or more employees. Title VII of this act prohibits employers from discriminating in hiring, advancement, wages, and other terms and conditions of employment on the basis of sex, race, color, religion, national origin, or sexual orientation or identity.

classical economists—A group of 18th and 19th century British economists who criticized mercantilism and believed that self-interest and competition promoted economic development. Adam Smith is often cited as the lead figure in this movement

classical model—A model of the economy in which it is assumed that prices, wages, and interest rates are flexible, so that all markets clear. In such an economy, all factors are fully employed, and the growth of output depends on the growth of available factor supplies. While many politicians continue to rely on this model, no reputable economist does.

Clayton Act—1914 U.S. federal antitrust law that makes it unlawful for businesses to engage in certain actions that are believed to lessen competition and to lead to monopolies. Four specific practices are made illegal: (1) price discrimination; (2) tying contracts in which the buyer must agree to deal exclusively with one seller and not to purchase goods from competing seller; (3) interlocking directorships in which memberships of boards of directors of two or more firms are almost identical; and (4) buying stock in a competing company when the purpose is to reduce competition.

closed corporation—One whose stock is not sold to the public.

closed economy—An economy that does not interact with other economies in the world.

closed shop—A firm in which the union controls hiring. A prospective worker must belong to the union in order to be hired. (Contrast with *union shop* and *open shop*.)

Coase theorem—A proposition, developed by Ronald Coase, that pollution and other externalities can be efficiently controlled through voluntary negotiations among the affected parties (polluters and those harmed by pollution).

coincident indicators—Economic variables, such as payroll employment, industrial production, personal income, and manufacturing and trade sales, that tend to change at the same time that real output changes.

coins—Government-issued pieces of metal that have value and are used as money.

collateral—Something with monetary value pledged as security for a loan.

collective bargaining—Negotiations with management by a union to prepare a labor contract.

collusion—A secret agreement entered into by two or more persons to perpetrate an illegal act.

colonialism—A system in which governments and economies are dominated by foreign powers.

command economy—An economy in which government controls virtually all allocation, production, and distribution of goods and services, e.g., USSR, North Korea, Cuba.

commercial bank—A bank that offers a range of deposit accounts, including checking, savings, and time deposits, and extends loans to individuals and businesses. Contrast with investment banking firms such as brokerages, which generally are involved in arranging for the sale of corporate or municipal securities.

commercial paper—Short-term notes issued by a corporation promising to repay a specified amount of money at a specified rate of interest.

committed cost—In accounting, a cost that results from a prior management decision and that cannot be changed quickly.

commodity—A comparatively homogeneous product that can typically be bought in bulk. It usually refers to a raw material—corn, oil, cotton, etc.—but can also describe a manufactured product used to make other things, e.g., microchips used in personal computers.

commodity money—Anything that serves both as money and as a commodity, e.g., gold and silver.

common market—A group of nations that have eliminated tariffs and other barriers that impeded trade with each other while maintaining a common external tariff on goods imported from outside the union.

common resources—Goods that are *rival* in consumption but not *excludable*.

common stock—A share in the ownership of a corporation with voting rights. An equity asset that represents an ownership share in a corporation and that usually entitles the owner to vote on the selection of directors and on other important company matters and also entitles the owner to receive dividends on the stock. Contrast with preferred stock.

Communism—Type of autocratic or state socialism in which a small unelected Communist party decides society's goals. (Contrast with small-c *communism*.)

communism—A form of political and economic organization based on the writings of Karl Marx and Friedrich Engels in which a single party controls the government, private property rights are abolished, and the people own resources in common. "Pure communism" is an economic system in which everyone willingly puts the common good first.

Communist Manifesto—*The Manifesto of the Communist Party*, written by Karl Marx and Friedrich Engels (1848), which sets out the principles of the Communist Party world wide.

comparative advantage—To be better suited to the production or one good than to the production of another good. Occurs when a country's producers have a lower opportunity cost of production of a good than another country. As long as the relative opportunity costs of producing goods differ among nations, there are potential gains from trade, even if one country has an absolute advantage in everything.

competition—Rivalry among buyers and among sellers in the purchase and sale of resources and products. Ability of individuals to freely enter into business activities.

competitive advantage—Something that gives a firm (or a person or a country) an edge over its rivals.

competitive, perfectly—A perfectly competitive market is one in which economic forces operate unimpeded. It must meet the following criteria: (1) Buyers and sellers are price takers; (2) The number of firms is large; (3) There are no barriers to entry or exit; (4) Firms' products are homogeneous (identical); (5) Exit and entry are instantaneous and cost free; (6) There is complete information available to everyone instantly; and selling firms are profit-maximizing entrepreneurial firms.

competitiveness—A country's ability to produce goods and services more cheaply than other countries.

complements—Two or more goods that are often consumed together. An increase in the price of one leads to a decrease in the demand for the other. Beds and bed sheets are complements. (Contrast with *substitutes*.)

compound interest—The type of interest that is earned on both the original principal amount and on the interest accumulated from earlier periods. Contrast with *simple interest*.

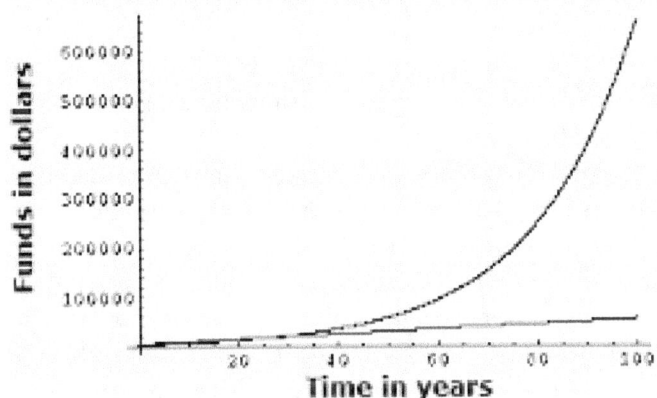

Growth of principal with compound interest

concentration ratio—The percentage of industry output that a
   specific number of the largest firms have. Example: If the
   four largest firms in an industry produce 80% of the
   market's output, that is a more highly concentrated industry
   than one in which the four largest firms produce 20%.
conditionality—Requirement of IMF loans that the developing
   country establish and implement responsible monetary and
   fiscal policies.
conglomerate—A large corporation whose activities span various
   unrelated industries.
conglomerate merger—Combination of unrelated businesses.
consequence—A result or effect of an action or decision; may be
   positive or negative.
constant dollars—Dollars adjusted for changes in purchasing
   power from a base year; value of dollars adjusted for
   inflation. Also called real dollars.

constant returns to scale—Technological forces that cause some firms' long-run average costs to remain constant as total product increases.

consume—To buy and use a good or service.

consumer confidence—How good consumers feel about their economic prospects.

consumer co-ops (cooperatives)—Retail businesses owned by members who share in the profits and who purchase goods and services at lower costs.

consumer credit report—Any communication of information by a consumer reporting agency that bears on a consumer's credit worthiness, credit standing, credit capacity, character, general reputation, personal characteristics, or mode of living and is obtained directly from the consumer's creditors or from the consumer. Also known as consumer report.

consumer economics—The study of economics that addresses decisions of consumers in the marketplace and personal money management.

consumer price index (CPI)—A measure of the cost of living as tabulated by the U. S. Bureau of Labor Statistics based on the actual retail prices of about 10,000 goods and services purchased by the typical consumer at a given time and compared to a base period that is changed from time to time. A CPI of 1.5 means that consumers are paying 50 percent more than they were paying during the base period for exactly the same basket of goods and services.

consumer sovereignty—Consumers' wishes control what business produces for sale. The right of the individual to make choices about what is consumed and produced.

consumer surplus—The difference between what consumers would have been willing to pay and what they actually pay. (Contrast with *producer surplus*.)

consumers—Members of households who use the goods and services that firms produce. People who buy goods and services for personal use.

consumption—The use of goods and services to satisfy human desires.

consumption expenditures (C)—Total spending by consumers on goods and services.

consumption function—A graph that shows how much consumption rises when disposable income rises.

consumption possibilities schedule—A schedule reflecting the alternative consumption possibilities available in an economy. In the absence of trade, the consumption possibilities schedule is the same as the production possibilities schedule.

consumption tax—A tax on expenditures, rather than on earnings. Consumption taxes are usually said to be "regressive," in that they constitute a higher percentage of a low-income-earning family than of a higher-income family.

contagion—The domino effect, such as when economic problems in one country spread to another. "When America sneezes, the rest of the world catches cold!"

contestable markets—Model of oligopoly that assumes that oligopolies act as perfectly competitive firms, even if little "real" competition exists, because existing firms fear new competition if they set prices too high.

contract law—A body of law that governs the requirements for forming a legally binding contract and that specifies the rights and duties of the parties to the contract.

convergence—A theory that countries become, or will continue to get, closer in terms of per capita income.

convertible currency—A currency that can be freely exchanged with currencies of other nations, e.g., U.S. dollars, euros, UK sterling, and yen.

cooperative (co-op)—An association of individuals or companies that perform business functions for their members.

copyright—Exclusive right of authors of original writing and artistic work to sell or reproduce their works for their lifetime plus 50 years.

corporate bonds—Certificates that corporations issue when they borrow money for long periods of time.

corporate takeover—Purchase of a firm by another firm or individual.

corporation—A business legally treated as a "person" and managed on behalf of its owners (stockholders), who are not liable for the actions of the corporate "person." Corporations are chartered by states and given legal status similar to that of a natural person. A legal entity that exists separately from its owners and that can enter into contracts, sue in court or be sued, own property, and engage in other business transactions.

correlation—Term in statistics meaning the joint movement of data points.

corroboration—Term in statistics meaning the data are more consistent with one theory than with any other theory.

cost—The value of everything a seller must give up in order to produce a good or service.

cost-benefit analysis (CBA)—Evaluating the merit of a proposed action by weighing its predicted benefits against its predicted costs.

cost minimization condition—When the ratio of marginal product to the price of an input is equal for all inputs.

cost of capital—The amount a firm must pay the owners of capital for the privilege of using it. This includes interest payments on corporate debt, as well as the dividends generated for shareholders.

cost-plus pricing—Theory of oligopoly that assumes firms set prices by marking them up by a certain percentage over their average cost.

cost-push inflation—Inflation caused by a general increase in production costs. (Contrast with *demand-pull inflation.*)

Council of Economic Advisers—A three-member group that gathers information on the economy, reports on economic developments, and recommends strategies to the President.

counterplanning—Process in a command economy that lets individuals low in the hierarchy influence the planning decisions of those above them in the hierarchy.

credit—A loan or delayed payment of an invoice. Enables one to enjoy the use of goods or services before paying for them.

credit agreement—A written promise to repay something that is borrowed.

credit card—A card that allows its holders to charge expenses. An open-ended credit arrangement in which a lender agrees to pay for goods and services purchased by a consumer and the consumer repays the lender in monthly payments at a specified rate of interest on the amount of the monthly outstanding balance.

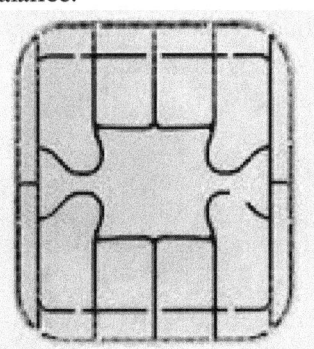

New credit cards come with an electronic security chip.

credit costs—Charges associated with the acceptance of a loan, including the finance charge and transaction fees (for example, loan fees, annual or monthly fees on a credit account).

credit crunch—When banks suddenly stop lending, or bond market liquidity evaporates, usually because creditors have become extremely risk averse.

credit default swap (CDS)—A financial exchange agreement that the seller of the CDS will compensate the buyer in the event of a loan default or other credit event. The buyer of the CDS makes a series of payments (the CDS "fee" or "spread") to the seller and, in exchange, receives a payoff if the loan defaults.

credit history—A record of past borrowing and repayments.

credit limit—Maximum amount of money that will be extended to a person by a financial institution or credit-card issuer.

credit record—See *credit report*, below.

credit report—A report about a person's credit history, including his or her ability and willingness to repay debts, based on how reliably he or she has repaid debts in the past. Also known as a credit record.

credit risk—The possibility of poor financial performance on the part of a business; also, the possibility that a borrower (an individual or a business) could be late with payments or could entirely fail to pay its obligations. Also known as default risk.

credit union—An association of affiliated people that offers to members insured savings plans and lending similar to commercial banks.

creditworthiness—The extent to which a person is deemed suitable to receive credit, especially as shown by reliability in repaying loans in the past.

creditor—One who lends money to another.

cross-price elasticity of demand—Percentage change in quantity demanded for one good divided by percentage change in price of a related good, everything else held constant. It measures the degree to which goods are substitutes or complements. When the cross-price elasticity of demand is positive, the goods are substitutes; when cross-price elasticity of demand is negative, goods are complements.

crowding in—The potential for government spending to stimulate private investment in an otherwise sluggish economy.

crowding out—The reduction in investment caused by expansionary fiscal policy's effect on interest rates.

currency—Paper money and coins issued by a government.

currency appreciation—A decrease in the number of units of a particular currency needed to purchase one unit of another currency. In such a case, the currency that has appreciated is said to have gotten "stronger."

currency board—A government organization existing in a few countries that establishes a fixed exchange rate for the nation's currency.

currency conversion—The process by which an amount of one nation's currency is exchanged for the currency of another country.

currency depreciation—An increase in the number of units of a particular currency needed to purchase one unit of another currency. In such a case, the currency that has depreciated is said to have gotten "weaker."

currency devaluation—When a government adjusts the value of the nation's currency so that it buys less of foreign currencies than before.

current account—The part of the balance of payments account that lists all short-term flows of payments.

current dollars—The value of dollars at a specified time and not adjusted for inflation. (Contrast with *constant dollars*.)

current ratio—A ratio that divides a company's current assets by its current liabilities to measure its short-term debt-paying ability.

customer service—The broad range of activities that a company and its employees undertake in order to keep customers satisfied so they will continue doing business with the company and speak positively about the company to other potential customers.

customer service representative (CSR)—Any person, other than a sales person, who provides support to customers face-to-face or through communications media.

customs union—A trade agreement among nations that imposes a common tariff on nonmember nations.

cyclical unemployment—Unemployment caused because there is insufficient GDP for jobs to be available to job seekers with employable skills.

❧ D ❧

DAX—A stock price index, based on stocks traded on the German Stock Exchange that is a commonly used indicator of the general trend in the prices of stocks and bonds in Germany.

deacquisition—One company's sale of parts of another company it has bought, often resulting in mass losses of jobs in the company being dismantled.

deadweight loss—The fall in total surplus that results from a market distortion, such as a tax.

debenture—An unsecured corporate bond for which the borrower does not pledge any assets or income as security.

debit—In accounting, a specified change made to the monetary value of an account. A debit increases the value of asset accounts and expense accounts, whereas it decreases the value of liability accounts, owners' equity accounts, and revenue accounts.

debt—An amount of money one owes to others.

debt-to-equity ratio—A financial ratio, calculated by dividing a company's total long-term debt by its total equity, that is helpful in determining a company's solvency.

decision-making lag—The time needed to decide what changes to make in government policy after a macroeconomic problem is identified.

decreasing returns to scale (diseconomies of scale)—Technological forces which cause some firms' long run average costs to rise as total product increases.

deep learning—A branch of machine learning based on a set of algorithms that attempt to model high-level abstractions in data by using a deep graph with multiple processing layers, composed of multiple linear and non-linear transformations.

default—Failure to meet a financial obligation when it comes
   due.
deficiency payment—A government payment to compensate
   farmers for all or part of the difference between product
   prices actually paid for a specific commodity and higher
   guaranteed target prices.
deficit—When expenditures exceed income.
deflation—A period of falling price levels. Opposite of inflation.
demand—Quantity of a good that will be bought at various
   prices; it is represented by the entire demand curve. The
   total quantity of goods and services consumers are willing
   and able to buy at all possible prices during some time
   period. (Contrast with *supply*.)
demand curve—Graphical representation of how much of a good
   will be bought at various prices.

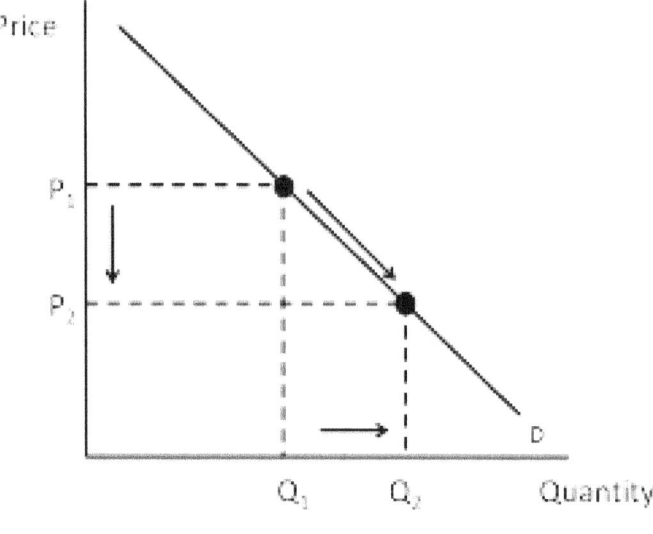

Demand curve

demand deposits—Checking accounts held by commercial banks that pay no interest. The largest component of the money supply (M1).

demand-pull inflation—Inflation caused when aggregate demand for products temporarily outstrips the capacity to increase production.

demand-side economics—Macroeconomic policy that focuses on changes in aggregate demand as a way of promoting full employment and price stability. (Contrast with *supply-side economics*.)

demerit goods or activities—Things government believes are bad for you, although you may like them: Example: Government may make using marijuana a crime, even though you may see no harm in the activity. (Contrast with *merit goods or activities*.)

democratic socialism—A socialist system that operates within the existing democratic framework.

deposit insurance—Government backing of bank deposits up to a certain amount. In the United States, that amount is currently $250,000.

depository institution—A financial services company, such as a commercial bank or thrift institution, that engages in the retail banking activities of accepting deposits from individuals and making loans.

depreciation—The total amount that the value of capital falls in a given time period. (Contrast with *appreciation*.)

depression—A severe decline in general economic activity in terms of magnitude and length. GDP growth is negative for at least two consecutive quarters and unemployment rises sharply. More severe than recession.

deregulation—Lifting of government controls over an industry.

derivative—An asset that derives its value from another asset. For example, a call option on the stock of Coca-Cola is a derivative security that obtains value from the shares of Coca-Cola that can be purchased with the call option. Call options, put options, convertible bonds, futures contracts, and convertible preferred stock are examples of derivatives. A derivative can be either a risky or low-risk investment, depending upon the type of derivative and how it is used.

derived demand—The demand for factors of production by firms, which depends on consumers' demands.

derived demand curve for labor—A demand curve showing the maximum amount of labor, measured in labor hours, that a firm will hire.

devaluation—A sudden fall in the value of a currency against other currencies.

developing countries—Nations typified by high rates of illiteracy, high unemployment, rapid population growth, and exports of primary products (raw minerals and agricultural products). Also called less developed countries (LDC).

development economics—A branch of economics concerned with issues of economic development in poor countries.

development expenses—Costs related to starting a new product or line of business.

differentiation—The process of making products unique.

diminishing marginal productivity, law of—As more and more of an input is added to an existing fixed input, eventually the additional output one gets from that additional input will fall.

diminishing marginal utility—When at some point the last item consumed will be less satisfying than the one before.

diminishing returns—The more you have, the smaller is the extra benefit you get from having even more; also known as *diseconomies of scale*.

direct cost—In accounting, a cost incurred for or physically traceable to one specific product, line of business, department, or other cost object. Contrast with *indirect cost.*

direct taxation—Taxes levied on the income or wealth of an individual or company. Contrast with *indirect taxation.*

discount bond—A bond that has a current market value that is lower than the bond's principal or par value. Contrast with *premium bond.*

discount rate—The interest rate paid by commercial banks to borrow funds from the central bank, usually to avoid reserve shortfalls.

discounted cash flow—A method used to estimate attractiveness of an investment. DCF analysis uses future cash flow projections and discounts them to arrive at a present value used to evaluate the potential for investment. If the value arrived at through DCF analysis is higher than the current cost of the investment, the opportunity may be a good one.

discouraged worker—A person who has dropped out of the labor force because of lack of success in finding a job; this person is not counted in the unemployment rate, which includes only people who are in the labor force and are seeking jobs.

discoveries—Discovery of new sources of raw materials can lead to a higher standard of living. We can also discover new methods of doing things. The discovery of new methods— new techniques and technologies—is called "technical progress." Many students of economic history believe that technical progress is the only source of continuing economic growth in the long run, and that all countries and societies that have experienced rising standards of living over long periods of time (as the European, East Asian, and North American societies have done) have done so because of continuing, progressive, technological change.

discretionary costs—Costs that are partially or wholly under the control of current management and are flexible components of a budget that can be changed as conditions change.

discretionary income—Money left after buying necessities.

discrimination—The practice of favoring an individual or group over another, usually for reasons that have nothing to do with ability. Different treatment of individuals because of physical or social characteristics.

diseconomies of scale—An increase in per-unit cost as a result of an increase in output. (See *average total cost* in the short and long runs.)

disequilibrium—When supply and demand in a market are not in balance. Contrast with *equilibrium*.

disinflation—A fall in the rate of inflation. This means a slower increase in prices but not a fall in prices, which is known as *deflation*.

disintermediation—Cutting out the middleman. Disintermediation has become a buzz word in financial services in particular, as competitive and technological changes have done away with the need for established intermediaries, such as banks and brokers.

disposable personal income (DPI)—Income available for spending and saving by households.

distribution—The movement of goods through channels of trade from producer to consumer.

distribution channel—See *distribution system*.

distribution system—In marketing, a network of organizations and individuals that performs all distribution activities. Also known as distribution channel. (See also *distribution*.)

district bank—One of 12 banks in the United States Federal Reserve System overseeing banking and credit in its geographical region.

diversification—Spreading risk. A defensive principle of investment portfolio construction that requires balancing the selection of portfolio assets among a variety of types of securities, industries, or nations.

dividend—Money earned on stock holdings; usually, it represents a share of profits paid in proportion to the share of ownership. Dividends paid in cash are called cash dividends. Dividends paid in the form of additional shares of stock are called stock dividends.

division of labor—Breaking down a large task into a series of small ones, so each worker completes one or a few of the steps involved in production. The idea, noted by Adam Smith in his 1776 book, *An Inquiry into the Nature and Causes of the Wealth of Nations,* that productivity is most advanced by specialization of work and of production by nations of those goods they can produce more efficiently than can other nations. Smith's insight is that cooperative production increases productivity: "The division of labor ... occasions, in every art, a proportionable increase in the productive powers of labor. ... It is the great multiplication of the productions of all the different arts, in consequence of the division of labor, which occasions, in a well-governed society, that universal opulence which extends itself to the lowest ranks of the people....In civilized society [one] stands at all times in need of the co-operation and assistance of great multitudes."

dollarization—When a country's own money is replaced as its citizens' preferred currency by the U.S. dollar.

domestic corporation-From the point of view of a particular state in the United States, a company that is incorporated under the laws of that state. Contrast with *alien corporation.*

dominant firm—A firm with the ability to set prices in its market.

double coincidence of wants—A situation in which two traders
are willing to exchange their products directly.

Dow Jones Industrial Average—A stock price index, based on 30
prominent industrial companies, a commonly used indicator
of general trend in prices of stocks in the U.S.

dual accounting—An accounting concept that states that every
financial transaction has two aspects—debits and credits—
that always equal each other.

dumping—Under national laws, sales of merchandise exported to
that nation from another at "less than fair market value,"
when such sales materially injure or threaten material injury
to producers of like merchandise in the importing nation.

duopoly—A market with two sellers. A subset of the oligopoly
form of market structure.

Dutch disease—The negative impact on an economy of anything
that gives rise to a sharp inflow of foreign currency, such as
the discovery of large oil reserves. The currency inflows
lead to currency appreciation, making the country's other
products less price competitive on the export market. It
also leads to higher levels of cheap imports and can lead to
deindustrialization as industries apart from resource
exploitation are moved to cheaper locations. The origin of
the phrase is the Dutch economic crisis of the 1960s
following the discovery of North Sea natural gas

dynamic laws of supply and demand—Phenomena involving the
interaction of supply and demand in markets. (1) When
quantity demanded is greater than quantity supplied, prices
tend to rise; when quantity supplied is greater than quantity
demanded, prices tend to fall. (2) The larger the difference
between quantity supplied and quantity demanded, the
greater the pressure to rise if there is excess demand or to
fall if there is excess supply. (3) When quantity supplied
equals quantity demanded, prices do not tend to change.

earnings—Profits. Sometimes called "net."

e-commerce—Promotion and sale of goods and services over the Internet.

econometrics—The application of statistical methods to economics. A model of some aspect of the economy is set up, stated in mathematical terms. The model is compared with available statistical facts about the economy.

economic forces—The forces of scarcity.

economic growth—An increase in a nation's capacity to produce goods and services.

economic indicator—Any of several measures of the condition of an economy.

economic decision rule—If benefits exceed costs, do it; if costs exceed benefits, don't do it.

economic imperialism—Domination of the economies of colonies by their rulers, or of politically independent countries by foreign or multinational companies.

economic institution—A physical or mental structure that significantly influences economic decisions.

economic model—A simplified representation of reality designed to capture the important elements of the relationship under consideration.

economic nationalism—See *protectionism.*

economic policy—Action to influence the course of economic events.

economic profit—Definition of profit used by economists that states profit is total implicit and explicit revenues minus total implicit and explicit costs. (Contrast with *accounting profit.*)

economic profits—Return on entrepreneurship above and beyond normal profits.

economic reasoning—Making decisions based on costs and
   benefits.
economic sanctions—A way of punishing errant countries, which
   is currently more acceptable than bombing or invading
   them. One or more restrictions are imposed on
   international trade with the targeted country in order to
   persuade the target's government to change a policy. May
   include limiting export or import trade; constraining
   investment; and preventing transfers of money involving
   citizens or the targeted government.
economics—The "dismal science," according to Thomas Carlyle,
   a 19th-century Scottish writer. It has been described in
   many ways, few of them flattering. The most concise, non-
   abusive, definition is the study of how society uses its
   scarce resources. The social science that examines how
   people choose to use limited or scarce resources in
   attempting to satisfy their unlimited wants.
   Lionel Robbins: "Economics is the science which
   studies human behavior as a relationship between ends and
   scarce means that have alternative uses."
   John Maynard Keynes also defined economics as a
   method: "The theory of economics does not furnish a body
   of settled conclusions immediately applicable to policy. It is
   a method rather than a doctrine, an apparatus of the mind,
   a technique of thinking, which helps it possessors to draw
   correct conclusions."
   Alfred Marshall's definition is a classic: "Economics is a
   study of mankind in the ordinary business of life; it
   examines that part of individual and social action which is
   most closely connected with the attainment and with the
   use of the material requisites of wellbeing. Thus it is on one
   side a study of wealth; and on the other, and more
   important side, a part of the study of man."

economic system—Set of economic institutions that determines
important economic decisions to resolve the questions of
what, how, and for whom resources are used.

economically efficient—Using the method of production that
produces a given level of output at the lowest possible cost.
(See *technical efficiency.*)

economies of scale—Reductions in unit costs resulting from
large-scale production. A decrease in per-unit cost as a
result of an increase in output.

economies of scope—The costs of producing products are
interdependent so that producing one good lowers the cost
of producing another.

economize—To get the most from one's resources.

economy—An institutional structure through which individuals
in a society coordinate their wants.

effective interest rate—Interest rate or rate of return that includes
the effects of compounding. Also known as the annual
percentage rate (APR). Contrast with nominal interest rate.
(See also *interest rate.*)

effectiveness lag—The time necessary for changes in monetary or
fiscal policy to have an effect on the economy.

efficiency—Achieving a goal as cheaply as possible. The
condition that exists when there is no way that resources
can be reallocated to increase the production of one good
without decreasing the production of another. (Contrast
with *equity.*)

efficiency wage theory—The idea that keeping wages above the
level required to attract a sufficient pool of workers makes
workers compete to keep their jobs and results in greater
productivity. Contrast with subsistence wage theory.

efficient market hypothesis—The price of a financial asset
reflects all information available and responds only to
unexpected news.

efficiently—At the lowest possible cost in total resources, without considering who pays those costs.

effluent fees—Charges imposed by government on pollution. One way of correcting for negative externalities.

EFT—See *electronic funds transfer*.

elastic—In general, if changes in variable A cause changes in variable B, then the relative change in B is greater than the relative change in A. In other words, small changes in variable A cause relatively larger changes in variable B: ($E_d > 1$). An elastic relationship between two variables is a very responsive, or stretchable, relationship. Contrast with inelastic.

elasticity—The relative response of one variable to changes in another variable. The phrase "relative response" is best interpreted as the percentage change. For example, the price elasticity of demand, one of the more important applications of this concept in economics, is the percentage change in quantity demanded measured against the percentage change in price. Other notable economic elasticities are the price elasticity of supply, income elasticity of demand, and cross elasticity of demand.

elastic, perfectly—Percent change in price is zero: (E_d = infinity).

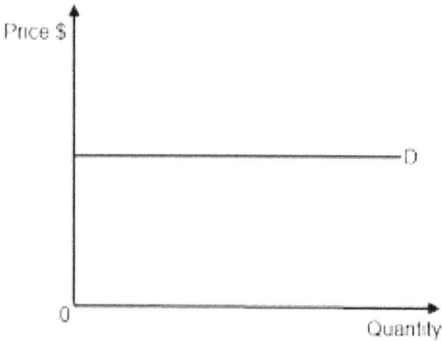

Perfectly elastic demand curve

electronic commerce (e-commerce)—Business conducted via the
    World Wide Web.
electronic funds transfer (EFT)—A method of transferring funds
    between financial intermediaries through an electronic
    computer network.
embargo—All-out restriction on import or export of a good.

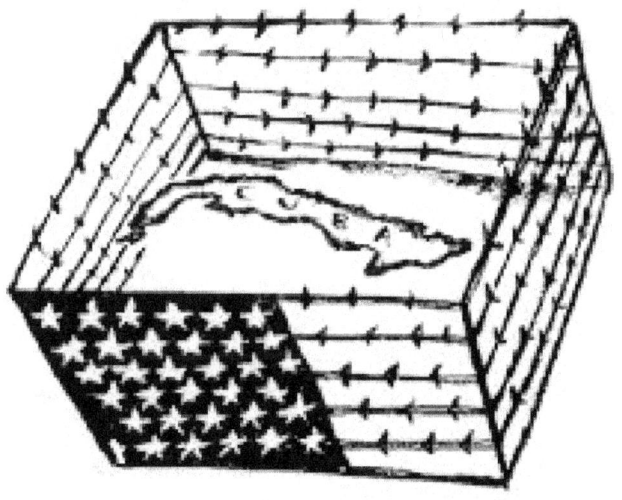

The U.S. has had an embargo against Cuba since 1962.

Employee Retirement Income Security Act (ERISA)—A U.S.
    federal law that regulates both employee welfare benefit
    plans, including group life and health insurance plans
    established by employers, and employer-sponsored
    retirement plans.
endogenous—Inside the economic model; the opposite of
    exogenous.
endogenous growth—Economic growth where the long-run
    growth rate is determined by the working of the system.
    Contrast with exogenous growth.

endogenous growth theory—A set of economic models and ideas that attempt to explain the rate of economic growth without recourse to the assumption that technological progress is simply given, and cannot be accounted for. Traditional growth models did tend to assume that technology - which they interpreted very widely to include everything from new machines, to a better understanding of efficient production methods or improved marketing techniques - is exogenous; that for all intents and purposes it is predetermined. Models of endogenous growth attempt to explain that technology.

endogenous variable—A classification of a variable generated by a statistical model that is explained by the relationships between functions within the model. For example, the equilibrium price of a good in a supply and demand model is endogenous because it is set by a producer in response to consumer demand.

Engel's law—People generally spend a smaller share of their budget on food as their income rises. The law was named after the statistician Ernst Engel (1821–1896).

entrepreneur—One who draws upon his or her skills and initiative to launch a new business venture with the aim of making a profit. Often a risk-taker, inclined to see opportunity when others do not.

entrepreneurship—Labor services that involve high degrees of organizational skills, concern, and creativity. The ability to organize and get something done. Imagination, innovative thinking, and management skills needed to start and operate a business. Sometimes considered a separate economic resource, but more often considered as part of the labor resource or human capital.

entropy—The notion, taken from thermodynamics, that "things fall apart."

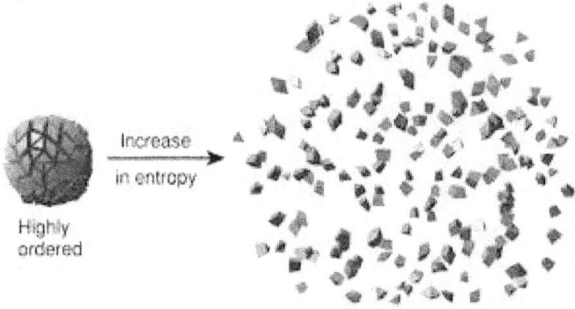

Model of an increase in entropy.

equation of exchange—The quantity of money (*M*) multiplied by its velocity (*V*) equals nominal income, which is the product of the price level (*P*) and real GDP (*Q*). $MV = PQ$.

equilibrium—Dynamic forces affecting a concept or an object cancel each other out. In a market economy, a stable market situation in which quantity demanded equals quantity supplied.

equilibrium price—Price toward which the invisible hand drives the market. The price at which the quantity of goods offered by suppliers equals the quantity taken by buyers. Market clearing price.

equilibrium quantity—The quantity of goods that will clear the market at the equilibrium price.

equity—(1) The capital of a firm, after deducting liabilities to outsiders other than shareholders, who are typically the legal owners of the firm's equity. This ownership right is the reason shares are also known as equities.

(2) Fairness; the concept of distributive justice used in welfare economics.

euro—The main currency of the European Union, launched in January, 1999, and in general circulation since 2002

eurodollars—U.S.-dollar denominated deposits at foreign banks or foreign branches of American banks. By locating outside of the United States, eurodollars escape regulation by the Federal Reserve Board.

Eurozone—19 of 28 nations in the European Union (EU) that use the euro as their currency.

evolutionary economics—A Darwinian approach to economics, sometimes called institutional economics. Following the tradition of Joseph Schumpeter, it views the economy as an evolving system and places a strong emphasis on dynamics, changing structures (including technologies, institutions, beliefs and behavior) and disequilibrium processes (such as innovation, selection and imitation).

excess burden—Loss caused to society when a policy results in society's losing income but suppliers failing to receive that income. Example: When farmers are constrained by a government program in how much they can produce, society loses income to higher prices but not all of that income is received by farmers but is simply wasted.

excess demand—Quantity demanded is greater than quantity supplied.

excess reserves—Reserves held by depository institutions in excess of required reserves.

excess returns—Getting more money from an economic investment than you needed to justify investing.

excess supply—Quantity supplied is greater than quantity demanded.

exchange controls—Limits on the amount of foreign currency that can be taken into a country, or of domestic currency that can be taken abroad.

exchange rate—The rate, or price, at which one country's
   currency is exchanged for the currency of another country.

exchange rate policy—Government policy of buying and selling a
   currency to affect its price.

excise tax—A tax on the manufacture or sale of a specific good
   or service.

excludable—The property of a good whereby a person can be
   prevented from using it. Also, see *rival*.)

	Rival?	
	Yes	**No**
Yes	Private Goods • Ice-cream cones • Clothing • Congested toll roads	Natural Monopolies • Fire protection • Cable TV • Uncongested toll roads
Excludable?		
No	Common Resources • Fish in the ocean • The environment • Congested nontoll roads	Public Goods • Tornado siren • National defense • Uncongested nontoll roads

Source: Mankiw, *Microeconomics.*

exogenous—Outside the model. Classical models of growth rely
   on an exogenous actor. An economy needs infusions of
   technological progress to grow. The rate of progress comes
   from outside the model; it is assumed by the modelers.
   New growth theory calculates the rate of progress inside the
   model by mapping its relationship to factors such as human
   capital, free markets, competition and government
   expenditure. Thus, in these models, growth is *endogenous*.

exogenous growth—Economic growth where the long-run
   growth rate is determined by factors outside the system, by
   population increase and an exogenously given rate of
   technical progress. Contrast with *endogenous* growth.

exogenous variable—A variable whose value is not determined within the set of equations, or models, established to make predictions or test a hypothesis.

expansion—In the business cycle, a period of six months or more of recovery after a downturn, when business and consumer spending increase and unemployment declines.

expansionary gap—The amount by which annual output in the short run exceeds the economy's potential output.

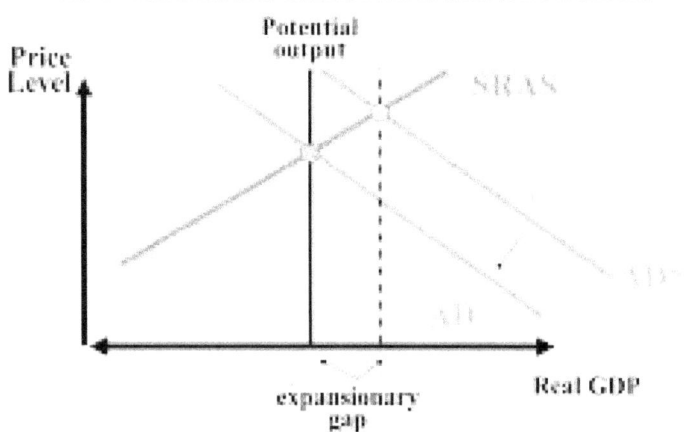

An Expansionary Gap Can be Closed by Contractionary Fiscal Policy

expectations—What people assume about the future when they make decisions. Economists debate whether people have irrational or *rational expectations*, or *adaptive expectations* that change to reflect learning from past mistakes.

expected returns—The capital gain plus income that investors think they will earn by making an investment, at the time they invest.

expenditure—Money that is spent.

expenditure approach—A method of calculating gross domestic product (GDP) that involves adding up expenditures on all final goods and services produced during the year. GDP = $C + I + G + (X - M)$, where C is consumption, I is gross private investment, G is government spending, and $(X - M)$ is net exports (exports minus imports).

expenditure tax—A tax on what people spend, rather than what they earn or their wealth. Examples are sales tax, value-added tax (VAT), and goods-and-services tax (GST).

expenses—Payments for goods and services.

experimental economics—The study of people's behavior in the marketplace by scientific testing in the laboratory.

explicit cost—The monetary payment a firm must make to obtain a resource.

export promotion—A development strategy that concentrates on producing for the export market.

exports—Goods and services that are produced domestically and sold to buyers in another country. (Contrast with *imports*.)

export subsidy—A lump sum given by a government for the purpose of promoting an enterprise considered beneficial to the public welfare. Such payments are generally banned by the World Trade Organization (WTO). (See *World Trade Organization*.)

external funds—Money from loans and other sources from outside the business, as opposed to funds created through business operations or investments. (Contrast with *internal funds*.)

externality—Effect of a trade or agreement on third parties that people did not take into account when they entered the trade or agreement. Benefits or costs of an activity that are borne by people not directly involved in the activity. (See *market failure*.)

❧ F ❦

face value—On a bond, the single payment at maturity promised by the issuer.

factor cost—A measure of output reflecting the costs of the factors of production used, rather than market prices, which may differ because of indirect tax and subsidy.

factor markets—Markets for inputs, or factors of production, that are used to produce outputs.

factors of production—Resources, or inputs, necessary to produce goods. Sometimes called land, labor, and capital. Sometimes, enterprise is considered a separate factor.

fad—A period of time during which, for reasons of fashion or over-optimism, financial investors are willing to pay more for a stock than its fundamental value.

Fair Labor Standards Act (FLSA)—In the United States, a federal law that establishes minimum wage, overtime pay, record keeping, and child labor standards that affect workers in most private companies and federal, state, and local governments.

fallacy of composition—The incorrect belief that what is true for the individual or part must necessarily be true for the group or whole. Example: A worker saves money and increases her bank account, so if all savers increased their savings, they would all have increased bank accounts. This is false reasoning, because if everyone increases their savings, consumption will fall, GDP will fall, and everyone will have less income, so total savings will fall.

farm lobby—An institution formed to further the political goals that will benefit farmers.

fast track—Procedures enacted by the United States Congress under which it votes within a fixed period on legislation submitted by the president to approve and implement international trade agreements.

feasible bundle—A bundle the consumer has the ability to
purchase; lies on or below the consumer's budget
constraint.

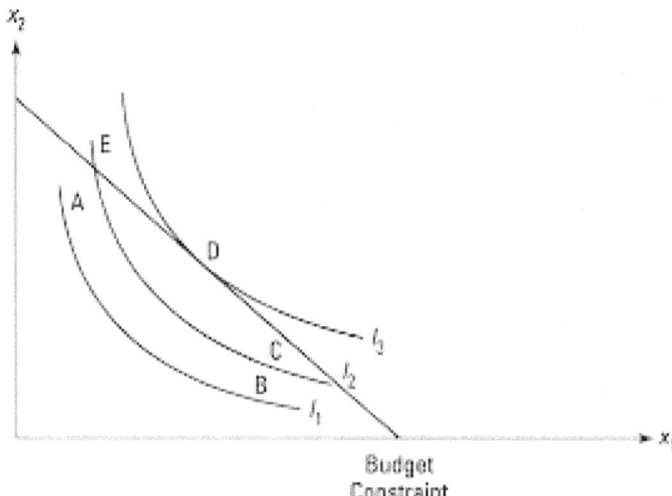

Budget
Constraint
All bundles are feasible, but I3 at D is optimal.

Fed—The United States Federal Reserve System.

Fed accommodation—A change in the money supply by the Fed
to maintain a constant interest rate in the face of changes in
money demand or in spending.

Federal Deposit Insurance Corporation (FDIC)—In the United
States, a federal agency that insures deposits made into
member banks and savings and loans up to $250,000 per
person/per institution.

federal funds market—A market for day-to-day lending and
borrowing of reserves among financial institutions. These
institutions borrow from one another in order to maintain
their required reserve ratio.

federal funds rate—The interest rate prevailing in the federal
funds market. (See above.)

Federal Reserve Bank—One of 12 operating arms of the United States Federal Reserve System, located throughout the nation that, together with their 25 branches, carry out various functions of the U.S. central bank system.

Federal Reserve System—The principal monetary authority (central bank) of the United States, which issues currency and regulates the supply of credit in the economy. It consists of a seven-member Board of Governors in Washington, D.C., 12 regional Federal Reserve Banks, and their 25 branches. Often referred to as "The Fed."

Federal Trade Commission (FTC)—A U.S. federal regulatory agency that enforces antitrust and trade practices laws. The FTC is empowered to, among other things: (1) prevent unfair methods of competition, and unfair or deceptive acts or practices in or affecting commerce; (2) seek monetary redress and other relief for conduct that injures consumers; (3) adopt trade regulation rules to define specific acts or practices that are unfair or deceptive and establish requirements designed to prevent such acts or practices; (4) conduct investigations relating to the organization, business, practices, and management of entities engaged in commerce; and (5) make reports and legislative recommendations to Congress.

Federal Unemployment Tax Act—Federal legislation in the United States that, when combined with individual state laws, provides covered individuals with protection against loss of income resulting from unemployment.

fertility of research—The degree to which spending on research and development translates into new ideas and new products.

feudalism—Political system divided into small communities in which a few powerful people protect those who are loyal to them.

fiat money—Money not useful as a commodity; its status as
　　money is conferred by the government and has no intrinsic
　　value as a commodity. (Contrast with *commodity money*.)

Example of fiat money

final goods and services—Goods and services sold to final, or
　　ultimate, users.
finance charge—The total amount one pays to use credit.
financial accounting—A field of accounting that focuses primarily
　　on reporting a company's financial information to meet the
　　needs of the company's external users.
financial intermediaries—Institutions that serve as go-betweens,
　　accepting funds from savers and lending those funds to
　　borrowers.
financial markets—Organizations in which savers exchange with
　　borrowers who are willing to pay for the use of the savers'
　　money.
financial planner—A professional who analyzes a client's financial
　　circumstances and goals and prepares a program, usually in
　　writing, to meet the client's financial goals.

financial planning—A coordinated process for identifying, planning for, and meeting goals related to financial needs for individuals, families, and small businesses.

financial statements—Standardized reports of a company's major monetary events and transactions.

firms—Organizations of individuals formed to transform factors of production into goods for consumers, governments, and other firms.

first dynamic law of supply and demand—When quantity demanded is greater than quantity supplied, prices tend to rise; when quantity supplied is greater than quantity demanded, prices tend to fall.

fiscal policy—The national government's decisions about the amounts of money it spends and collects in taxes to achieve full employment and a non-inflationary economy. Implemented by the Congress and the President. (Contrast with *monetary policy.*)

fiscal year—A 12-month accounting period chosen by a company for financial reporting purposes. Contrast with calendar year.

fixed costs—Costs that remain the same in the period of time under consideration and cannot be changed regardless of how much business a firm does.

fixed exchange rate system—A system in which exchange rates between currencies are set at a predetermined level and do not move in response to changes in supply and demand for various currencies. The government chooses an exchange rate and offers to buy and sell currencies at that rate.

fixed inputs—Inputs that cannot be changed in the short run.

flat tax—A simple tax system that would eliminate most deductions and apply the same tax rate to all incomes. Considered by nearly all economists to be a regressive tax and an impractical idea.

flexible exchange rate—Determination of exchange rates is left totally up to the market.

floating exchange rate system—A flexible system in which the exchange rate is determined by market forces of supply and demand, without government intervention.

Food for Peace—A program that provides for the disposition of U.S. farm products outside the United States.

FOOD
FOR
PEACE

foreign aid—Funds that are loaned or given to developing countries by developed countries.

foreign corporation—(1) From the point of view of any state in the United States, an insurance company that is incorporated under the laws of another state. (2) In Canada (and other nations), a company that is incorporated under the laws of another country. Also known as *nonresident corporation*.

foreign direct investment (FDI)—Investing directly in production in another country, either by buying a company there or establishing new operations of an existing business.

foreign exchange (FOREX)—Sale and purchase of currencies; any foreign currency.

foreign exchange rate—Number of units of foreign currency that trade for a unit of domestic currency.

forward contracts—Limited time agreements in which a seller promises to deliver a specified investment to a buyer sometime in the future for a price that is specified in the agreement. See also *futures contracts*.

fractional reserve banking system—A banking system in which a portion of deposits in the depository institutions are backed up by reserves. In the US, that portion is 10 percent.

franchise—A license to operate an individually owned business in a specific geographic area as if it were part of a large chain.

fraud—An act by which someone intentionally deceives another party and induces that other party to part with something of value.

free enterprise system—Economic system characterized by private ownership of property and productive resources, the profit motive to stimulate production, competition to ensure efficiency, and forces of supply and demand to direct production and distribution of goods and services.

free rider—Person who participates in something for free because others have paid for it.

free rider problem—The unwillingness of individuals to share in the cost of a public good.

free trade—The absence of tariffs and regulations designed to curtail or prevent trade among nations.

free trade association—Group of countries that allows free trade among its members with common barriers against the goods of other countries.

frictional unemployment—Temporary unemployment of people as they look for better jobs, graduate from school, etc.

fringe benefit—An indirect, non-cash benefit provided by employers in addition to regular wage or salary; e.g., health insurance, life insurance, profit-sharing, vacation, sick leave, parental leave, etc.

From each according to his ability, to each according to his need—Marxist theory of equity in production and distribution.

FTSI—A stock price index, based on stocks traded in Great Britain as calculated by the *Financial Times*, commonly used indicator of trend in prices of stocks and bonds in Britain.

full employment—The level of employment when there is no cyclical unemployment.

full employment unemployment rate—The unemployment rate when cyclical unemployment is eliminated.

full employment (potential) GDP—The level of GDP at which cyclical unemployment is eliminated.

full faith and credit—A phrase used to describe the unconditional guarantee or commitment by one entity to back the interest and principal of another entity's debt.

fungible—Something is fungible when any one single specimen is indistinguishable from any other. Somebody who is owed $1 does not care which particular dollar she gets.

futures—Contracts that require delivery of a commodity at a specified price on a specified future date.

future value (FV)—The value of a sum of money, invested at a specified interest rate, at the end of a given period of time. Contrast with present value (PV).

futures contracts—Limited-time agreements that give the owner of the agreement the right to buy or sell a specified investment in the future for a price that is set through trading on an organized exchange.

❧ G ❧

GAAP accounting records—Accounting records that focus on showing the company's financial stability along with its profitability. Designed for financial reporting to investors and the public at large, GAAP accounting records are prepared according to generally accepted accounting principles. Contrast with statutory accounting records.

game theory—Analyzes oligopolistic behavior as a complex series of strategic moves and reactive countermoves among rival firms.

GDP—Gross domestic product, a measure of economic activity in a country. It is calculated by adding the total value of a country's annual output of goods and services. GDP = private consumption (C) + investment (I) + government spending (G) + exports – imports (X – M).

GDP deflator—A measure of the average nominal price level of all final goods and services produced in the economy.

gearing—A company's debt expressed as a percentage of its equity; also known as *leverage*.

General Agreement on Tariffs and Trade (GATT)—Enacted in 1947, and effective in 1948, an organ of the United Nations and an international agreement not to impose trade restrictions except under certain limited conditions. Replaced in 1995 by World Trade Organization (WTO).

general equilibrium analysis—Analysis of simultaneous interaction of all markets.

generally accepted accounting principles (GAAP)—A set of financial accounting standards that all publicly traded companies in the United States and all companies in Canada follow when preparing their financial statements. Contrast with statutory accounting practices.

Giffen good—A product that people consume more of as the price rises and vice versa, violating the law of demand.

Gini coefficient—Named for Italian statistician and sociologist
    Corrado Gini, a measure of inequality in the distribution of
    income or wealth. In a Lorenz curve, the Gini coefficient is
    the ratio of the area between the diagonal and the Lorenz
    curve to the total area under the diagonal. The larger the
    Gini coefficient, the more inequality there is in the
    economy. (See *Lorenz curve.*) In the United States, the Gini
    tends to increase under Republican administrations and
    decrease under Democratic administrations.

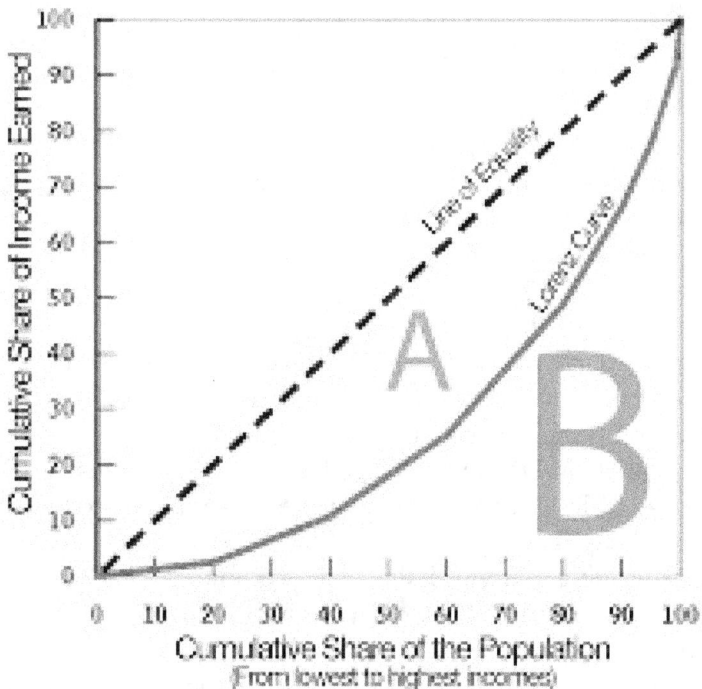

*The Gini coefficient is equal to the area marked A divided by (A+B). When
disparity increases, A increases; i.e., the Lorenz curve becomes more bowed.*

glasnost—The greater willingness of what had been the Soviet government to allow the Soviet people and the rest of the world to know what was going on in the Soviet Union. The policy was initiated under the leadership of then premier Mikhail Gorbachev.

global warming theory—Theory that the earth is going through a period of warming due to the rise of carbon dioxide gases caused by the burning of fossil fuels. Some scientists prefer the term "climate change," which takes into account not only warming but other severe discontinuities in global climate conditions.

gold standard—A monetary system in which currencies are defined in terms of a given weight of gold.

good-bad paradox—The phenomenon of doing poorly because you are doing well. Example: Wheat farmers work hard and have a good harvest; because the supply of wheat is large, prices received by the farmers fall.

goods—Anything that satisfies human needs. **Tangible** goods are material possessions that have physical substance. Finished goods are those ready for use by end users. Intermediate goods are items that will be transformed into another product by means of production. **Intangible** goods have no physical substance, e.g., entertainment.

government—Combination of federal, state, and local agencies whose officials are elected by the people or appointed by elected officials.

government bonds—Bonds issued by governments—including federal, state, provincial, county, city, and local governments. See also *bonds*.

grandfather in—To pass a law affecting a specific group but providing that those already in the group before the law was passed are not subject to the law.

Great Depression—A decade of high unemployment and
negative economic growth in the U.S. and other nations
covering the 1930s.

Outdoor soup kitchen in the Great Depression

Gresham's Law—"Bad money drives out good." If there are two
forms of commodity money accepted by law as having
similar face value, the more valuable commodity will
disappear from circulation. Named by Henry Dunning
Macleod, later made Sir Thomas Gresham (1519–1579).

gross domestic product (GDP)—Total value of all final goods
and services produced *in an economy.*

gross national product (GNP)—Total value of all final goods and
services produced *by a nation's citizens*, regardless of where
the activities take place. Generally replaced by GDP as a
measure of economic activity.

gross private investment (*I*)—Total purchases of capital and new
housing by the private sector, plus increases in inventories.

Group of Five (G5)—A group of five wealthy nations that meet
to try to coordinate their economic policies: Britain, France,
Germany, Japan, and United States.

Group of Seven (G7)—A group of seven wealthy nations that
meet to try to coordinate economic policies: G5 plus Italy
and Canada. (Russia has pressed to be included in a "Group
of Eight.")

❧ H ❧

Habakkuk thesis—Proposed and named after British economist, Sir John Habakkuk, the notion that high wages and labor scarcity stimulated technological progress in the U.S. in the 1800s, and in particular brought about the American system of manufacturing based on interchangeable parts.

hard currency—Money that can be converted to other currencies in most countries. Hard currencies are used for international transactions and national bank reserves.

health maintenance organization (HMO)—A health care plan that combines the financing and delivery of health care to provide comprehensive health care services for subscribing members in a particular geographic area in exchange for a prepaid fee.

hedging—An investment strategy that combines different types of securities in a given investment portfolio in order to reduce the overall risk of the portfolio's asset mix.

Hedonic—Of or relating to utility. (Literally, pleasure-related.) A hedonic econometric model is one where the independent variables are related to quality; e.g. the quality of a product that one might buy or the quality of a job one might take. A hedonic model of wages might correspond to the idea that there are compensating differentials, that workers would get higher wages for jobs that were more unpleasant.

Herfindahl index—Named for Swedish economist Orris C. Herfindahl, a way to classify how competitive an industry is. It is calculated by adding the squared value of the market shares of all the firms in the industry. The higher the sum, the more concentrated (less competitive) the industry.

historical cost—Cost in terms of money actually spent. In accounting and investing, original purchase price of an asset.

homo economicus—The economist's model of human behavior.

homogeneous product—A product in which each unit of output is indistinguishable from any other unit of output. Example: refined sugar.

horizontal merger—Companies in the same industry merging together. (Contrast with *vertical merger*.)

hostile takeover—A merger in which one company buys another whose managers or board do not want to sell.

households—Groups of individuals (usually a family) living together and making joint decisions. The basic unit of the economy that provides resources to firms, earns incomes from those resources, makes consumption expenses, and produces savings.

household income tax rate—The average percentage of national income that government collects in personal income taxes.

housing wealth—The value of the housing stock.

human capital—The health, strength, education, training, and skills people bring to their jobs. Anything we do to change ourselves to make us more productive in the future, or we benefit from in other ways, is an investment in human capital. An obvious example is education. Another example is preventive health care. When we get health care that keeps us healthy in the future, so that we miss fewer days of work and are more productive (and enjoy life more in the future), that is an investment in human capital.

human resources—The function within a business organization that monitors the availability of qualified workers; recruits and screens applicants for jobs; helps select qualified employees; plans and presents appropriate orientation, training, and development for each employee; and administers employee benefit programs.

hyperbolic discounting—Tendency of people to place much greater importance on the immediate present then even the near future when making economic decisions.

hyperinflation—A period of rapidly rising price levels when the value of a nation's currency plummets in a short time.

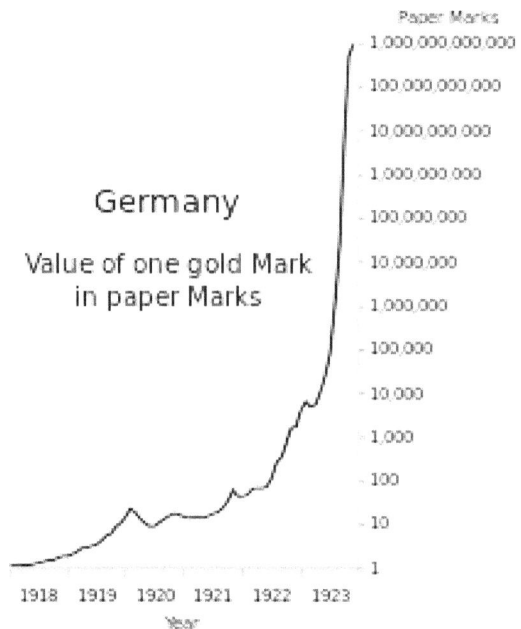

Hyperinflation in Germany in the 1920s

❧ I ❧

ideology—Values held so deeply that they are not questioned, e.g., religious, political, cultural.

imperfect competition—Markets in which sellers have more freedom to determine prices than in pure (or perfect) competition but less freedom than in a monopoly.

implementation lag—The time needed to introduce a change in monetary or fiscal policy.

implicit collusion—Multiple firms making the same pricing decisions even though they have not consulted with one another. Activity that appears to be illegal price-fixing may be strategic pricing, each firm taking account of what the other firms do.

import substitution—A development strategy that emphasizes manufacturing products that are currently imported.

imports—Goods or services produced in another country and sold domestically. (Contrast with *exports*.)

incentive-compatible contract—An agreement in which the incentives and goals of both parties match as closely as possible.

incentive effect—How much a person will change his or her hours worked in response to a change in the wage rate.

incentives—Reasons for doing something. In market economies, profit, interest, wages, and rents provide economic incentives.

income—Payments received plus changes in the value of assets in a specified time period.

income approach—A method of calculating GDP that involves adding up all payments to owners of resources used to produce output during the year.

income effect—A fall in the price of a good increases consumers' real income, making them more able to purchase all normal goods, so the quantity demanded increases.

income elasticity of demand—Percentage change in quantity demanded, divided by percentage change in income.

income-expenditure model—A graph that measures real income on the horizontal axis and aggregate spending on the vertical axis to determine the equilibrium quantity of aggregate output demanded.

income-leisure constraint—Shows combinations of income and leisure (non-paying activity) possible for a household.

income statement—A summary of a firm's revenues, costs, and taxes over a period of time. A financial document that provides information on a business organization's revenues and expenses during a specified period and indicates whether the business experienced a net income or net loss during the period. Also known as statement of operations.

income tax—An assessment levied by government on the net income of individuals and businesses.

increasing returns to scale (economies of scale)—Technological forces that cause some firms' long run average costs to fall as total product increases.

index—A statistical measurement system that tracks the performance of a group of similar investments.

index number—A measure of value compared to a base number.

indifference curve—A set of points, each representing a combination of some amount of good A and some amount of good B, that all yield the same amount of total utility.

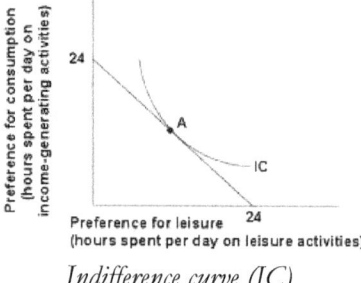

Indifference curve (IC)

indifference map—A set of indifference curves representing each possible level of total utility that can be delivered by a particular consumer from the consumption of two goods.

indirect business taxes—Federal, state, and local taxes and fees levied on products, e.g., fuel, liquor, and cigarette taxes.

indirect cost—In accounting, a cost that cannot be physically traced to one specific product, line of business, department, or other cost object. Also known as overhead costs. Contrast with direct cost.

indirect taxation—Taxes that do not come straight out of a person's pay packet or assets, or out of company profit. For example, a consumption tax, such as value-added tax. (See *expenditure tax*). Contrast with direct taxation, such as income tax. Indirect taxation has become increasingly popular with politicians because it may be less noticeable to people paying it than income tax and is harder to avoid paying.

individual retirement account (IRA)—An account set up at a financial institution that allows an individual to save for retirement with tax-free growth or on a tax-deferred basis.

indivisible setup cost—The cost of an indivisible input (one that cannot be divided into smaller units) for which a certain minimum amount of production must be undertaken before the input becomes economically feasible to use.

industrial organization—An applied field of economics, a specialization within microeconomics, which concentrates on the operation of individual industries.

industrial policy—Government's formal policy toward business. Usually refers to an active role by government in promoting particular industries with the aim of increasing exports.

industrial (or labor) relations—The study of the employment relationship between labor and management.

Industrial Revolution—Period c. 1750-1900 during which technology and machines rapidly modernized industrial production. The emergence of the factory system of production in which workers were brought together in one plant and supplied with tools, machines, and materials with which they worked in return for wages. The Industrial Revolution was spearheaded by rapid changes in the manufacture of textiles, particularly in England between 1750 and 1830. More broadly, the term applies to continuing structural change in the world economy.

industry—A group of business enterprises that produce similar goods, e.g., automobiles, or provide similar services, e.g., transportation.

inelastic—In general, if changes in variable A cause changes in variable B, then the relative change in B is less than the relative change in A. In other words, large changes in variable A cause relatively smaller changes in variable B. (E_d < 1). Contrast with *elastic*.

inelastic, perfectly—Percent change in quantity is zero: (E_d = 0).

infant industry argument—With initial protection, an industry will be able to become competitive.

inferior good—A good whose demand falls when buyers' incomes rise. Cheaper cuts of meat are inferior goods.

inflation—A rate of increase in the general price level of all goods and services during a specified period. (This is not to be confused with increases in the prices of specific goods relative to the prices of other goods.) During this period, the value of the nation's currency declines.

inflation risk—The risk that the average price level of goods and services will increase during a specified period.

informal sector—That part of the economy that is neither controlled nor measured, e.g., volunteer work, work for cash "under the table, homemaking, or criminal activity.

information systems—The function in an organization that facilitates data processing and enables the resulting information to be made available to employees who need it. Also known as information technology (IT).

infrastructure—Basic facilities, such as roads, harbors, water, and electricity, on which the smooth operation of the economy depends.

injection—Any payment of income other than by firms or any spending other than by domestic households, e.g., exports, investment, government purchases, and transfer payments.

input—Resources used in the production of a firm's output. This term is most frequently associated with the analysis of short-run production, and is often modified by the terms fixed and variable, as in fixed input and variable input. In the short run, the quantity of a fixed input cannot be changed, meaning it cannot be used to expand output. In contrast, a variable input can be changed, making it *the* means of expanding output in the short run.

inside director—A member of an organization's board of directors who holds a position with the company in addition to the position on the board. Contrast with *outside director.*

insolvency—The inability of a business organization to pay its financial obligations as they come due.

institutional economics—Focuses on understanding the role of institutions in shaping economic behavior. Emphasizes a broader study of institutions and views markets as a result of the complex interaction of these various institutions (e.g. individuals, firms, states, and social norms).

insurance—Protection from financial losses from emergencies and accidents. A mechanism for transferring the risk of financial loss from events such as fire, accident, illness, or death from an individual or entity to an insurance company.

intangible asset—An asset representing ownership of a legal right or other nonphysical resource, e.g., patents, trademarks, copyrights, business methodologies, trade secrets, goodwill, celebrity endorsements, contracts with sports teams (whose members wear a company's logo on their uniforms), and brand recognition. Contrast with tangible asset.

intellectual property—Ownership, as evidenced by patents, trademarks, and copyrights, conferring the right to possess, use, or dispose of products created by human ingenuity.

interest—Payment for using someone else's money; income from allowing someone to use one's capital.

interest rate—The percentage by which an amount of money is multiplied to derive the amount that is paid for the use of that money; often expressed in decimal form.

intermediate goods and services—Goods and services purchased for further processing and resale.

internal accounting records—Accounting records designed for financial reporting to company management, whose main interest is in having appropriate data for making decisions.

internal audit—An examination of a company's records, policies, and procedures that is conducted by the company's own employees to ensure that service standards are met, data recorded in the company's files is accurate and complete, and established procedures are being followed. Contrast with external audit

internal funds—Income, such as profit, that comes from business operations or investments. (Contrast with *external funds*.)

internal rate of return (IRR)—In investments, the percentage rate at which an asset's earnings must be discounted, using present value techniques, in order to exactly repay the initial investment in the asset. For investments in insurance products, also known as return on investment (ROI).

Internal Revenue Service (IRS)—A part of the United States
Department of the Treasury responsible for enforcing the
provisions of laws and regulations concerning income taxes
in the United States.

International Bank for Reconstruction and Development—The
World Bank, along with the International Monetary Fund,
financial institutions established at the end of World War II
at Bretton Woods, New Hampshire, USA, to assist nations
to rebuild and to restore and maintain financial stability.

International Monetary Fund (IMF)—A multinational financial
institution concerned primarily with monetary issues.

inventory—Stock of goods held by a business. In accounting, an
itemized count and listing of a company's assets, such as
property, products, materials, or securities.

investment—The purchase of capital equipment or expenditures
on human capital that will be used to produce goods or
services. Also, in financial terms, the purchase of a security,
such as a stock or bond.

investment demand curve—The relation between the market rate
of interest and the quantity of investment demanded in the
economy, other things constant.

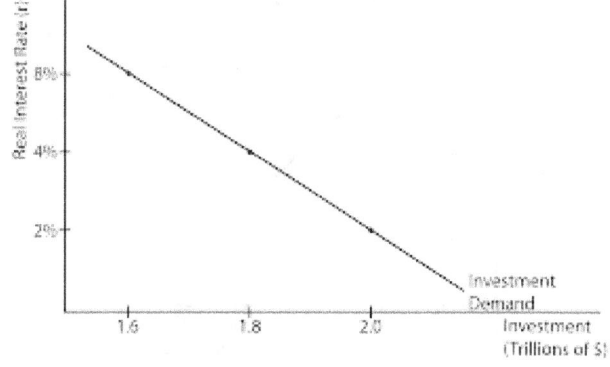

Investment Demand Curve

investment function—The relation between planned investment and the level of income, other things constant.

investment-grade bond—A bond that rated by an investment advisory firm as having a low probability of default.

invisible foot—Political and legal forces that guide our actions.

invisible hand—Economic forces that guide our actions. Adam Smith's idea that free markets restrain prices to some "natural" level and assure the supply of goods and services at the "natural" price.

invisible hand theory—The market will coordinate individuals' decisions.

invisible handshake—A term coined by Brookings Institution economist Arthur Okun to describe social and historical forces that guide our actions and modify choices determined only be the "invisible hand" of Adam Smith.

IS-LM model—(Investment-Saving /Liquidity preference-Money supply). A macroeconomic tool that shows the relationship between interest rates and real output in the goods and services market and the money market (also known as the assets market and Hicks–Hansen model.)

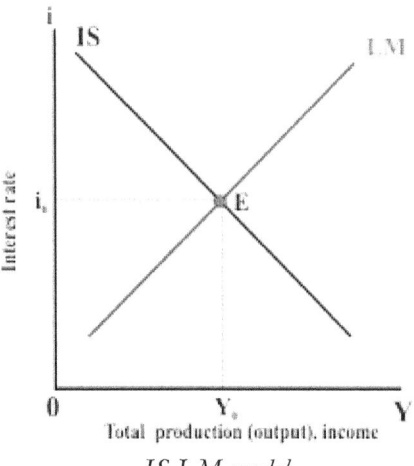

IS-LM model

⊱ J ⊰

J-curve—Curve describing the rise and fall in the balance of trade deficit following a fall in the exchange rate. The shape of the trend of a country's trade balance following a devaluation. A lower exchange rate initially means cheaper exports and more expensive imports, making the current account worse (a bigger deficit or smaller surplus). After a while, the volume of exports will rise because of lower price to foreign buyers, and domestic consumers buy fewer costlier imports. Eventually, the trade balance will improve on what it was before the devaluation. If there is a currency appreciation there may be an inverted J-curve.

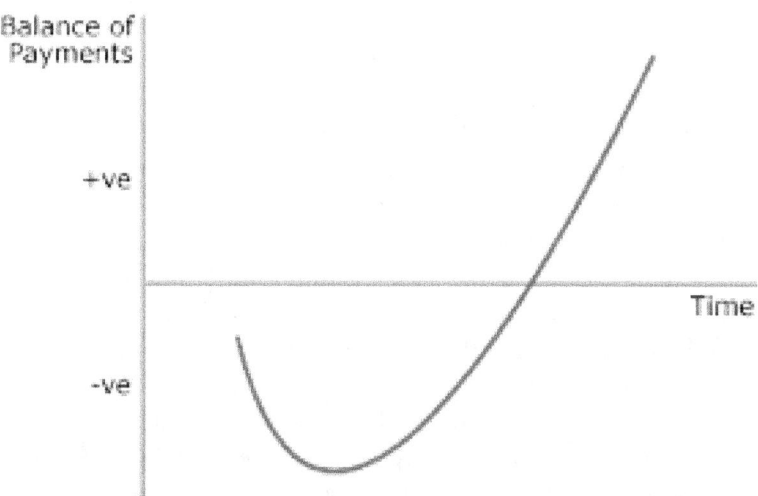

The "J curve" refers to the trend of a country's trade balance following a devaluation or depreciation under a certain set of assumptions.

JEL Classification Codes—A classification system for books and journal articles relevant to the economic researcher. Originated by the *Journal of Economic Literature.*

job lock—The situation of a person with a U.S. job who is not free to leave for another job because the first job has medical benefits associated with it that the person needs, and the second one would not, perhaps because "pre-existing conditions" are often not covered under U.S. health insurance.

Job Market—A market in which employers search for employees and employees search for jobs. The job market is not a physical place as much as a concept demonstrating the competition and interplay between different labor forces. The job market can grow or shrink depending on the labor demand and supply within the overall economy, specific industries, for specific education levels or specific job functions.

job search—The time it takes to find a job.

jobless claims—The number of people who are filing or have filed to receive unemployment insurance benefits, as reported weekly by the U.S. Department of Labor.

joint supply—Some products or production processes have more than one use. For instance, cows can both provide milk and be eaten. If farmers increase the number of cows they own in response to an increase in demand for milk, they are also likely to increase, a little later, the supply of meat, causing beef prices to fall.

journals—In the context of research economics journals are academic periodicals, usually with peer-reviewed contents. A comprehensive list of journals is at http://economics. about.com/gi/dynamic/offsite.htm?site=http://www.helsi nki.fi/WebEc/

just-in-time—A system of inventory management in which suppliers provide materials as they are needed and producers meet demand for finished goods without stockpiling inventory.

✎ K ✎

Keogh plan—In the United States, a qualified individual retirement arrangement (IRA) that allows self-employed persons to deposit a portion of their income earned from self-employment into a tax-deferred savings plan. Also known as HR 10 plan. See also *individual retirement arrangement* (IRA).

keiretsus—Japanese system of vertically and horizontally integrated firms.

key person—Any person or employee whose continued participation in a business is necessary to the success of the business and whose death or disability would cause the business a significant financial loss.

Keynes, John Maynard—British economist whose ideas profoundly affected the theory and practice of modern macroeconomics, as well as the economic policies of governments. He greatly refined earlier work on the causes of business cycles, and advocated the use of fiscal and monetary measures to mitigate the adverse effects of economic recessions and depressions.

John Maynard Keynes (1883-1946)

Keynesian—A view of the economy modeled on that of John
Maynard Keynes that a capitalist economy has the capacity
to remain for long periods in a short-term equilibrium
involving substantially lower output than would be
consistent with full employment. Contrasted with the
classical model, Keynesians believe output is to a large
extent determined by aggregate demand, so the level of
output can be affected by monetary and fiscal policies.
Nearly all reputable economists today are, to some extent,
Keynesians, a notable exception being extremists like
Milton Friedman, who continued to believe government
has virtually no useful role in the economy—a position he
renounced just prior to his death.

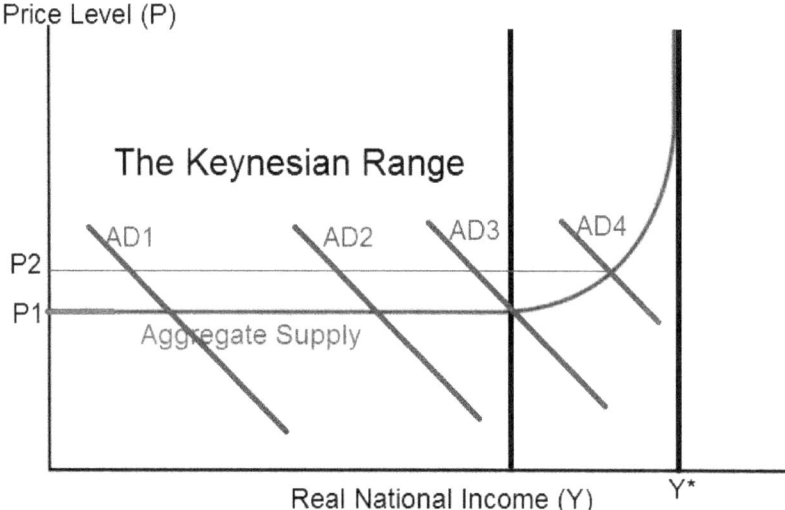

Keynesian cross diagram—Demonstrates the relationship
  between aggregate demand (shown on the vertical axis) and
  aggregate supply (shown on the horizontal axis, measured
  by output). In the diagram, the equilibrium level of output
  and demand is determined where the desired spending
  curve intersects a line that represents the equality of total
  income and output (AD=Y). The intersection gives the
  equilibrium real output, Y.

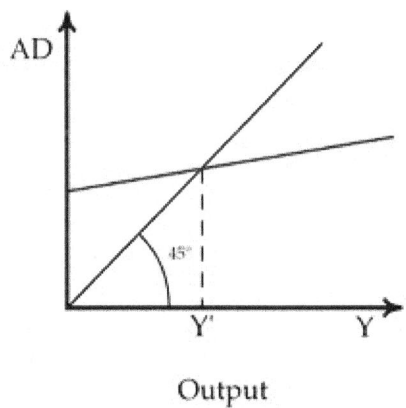

Output

The Keynesian Cross

kinked demand curve—Model of oligopoly which assumes that
  rival firms will match any price reduction, but will not
  match any price increase.

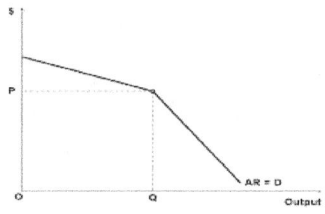

Kinked demand curve

kleptocracy—Corrupt, thieving government, in which the politicians and bureaucrats in charge use the powers of the state to feather their own nests. Russia in the years immediately after the fall of communism was a clear-cut example, with Mafia-friendly government members allocating themselves valuable shares during the privatization of state-owned companies, accepting bribes from foreign businesses, not collecting taxes from "helpful" companies and siphoning off international aid into their personal offshore bank accounts. (*The Economist*)

Kondratiev cycle—Proposed by Nikolai Kondratiev, a Russian economist, a theoretical long cycle in economic activity with a period of 60 or more years. Also called Kondratiev wave, supercycles, great surges, long waves, K-waves, or the long economic cycle). Sinusoidal-like cycles in the modern capitalist world economy. Averaging fifty and ranging from approximately forty to sixty years in length, the cycles consist of alternating periods between high sectoral growth and periods of relatively slow growth. Unlike the short-term business cycle, the long wave of this theory is not well accepted by current mainstream economics.

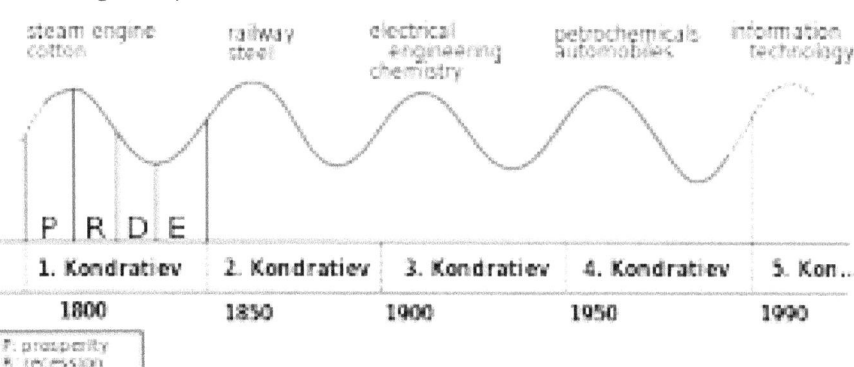

Kondratiev waves

❧ L ❧

labor—The physical and mental effort of humans. An economic resource, along with land and capital, used to produce goods and services. We may not think of labor as a resource, and of course it differs from the other two categories, since labor is directed human action and thus requires that the human being have some motivation. (Money is one possible motivation, of course, and a common one). Land does not require motivation. But, from several points of view, labor is the most important resource. From the point of view of cost, it is quite important. In the American economy, labor costs amount to something between two-thirds and three-quarters of costs (net of raw materials). Labor is also important to most of us because it is the resource from which we expect to get our living.

labor economics—A specialization within microeconomics that studies the economics of labor markets; it has some macroeconomic aspects.

labor force—The total number of people employed or looking for work. To be a member of the labor force, one must be working for pay, or be officially unemployed. Excludes full-time students, military and, prisoners.

labor force participation rate—The ratio of the number in the labor force to the population of working age.

labor intensive—A production process that involves comparatively large amounts of labor. Contrast with capital intensive.

labor market—Factor market in which individuals supply labor services for wages to firms that demand labor services.

labor productivity—The amount a work force can produce in a given time. Average output per worker.

labor unions—Associations of workers formed to promote the interests of their members.

Laffer curve—A politically inspired model of dubious credibility proposed by Arthur Laffer to Ronald Reagan that purports to show lower tax rates on the rich will result in greater total tax revenues to the government. Discredited policy of Reagan's administration, which cut taxes on the rich and tripled the national debt. (Often called "Laugher curve.")

The Laffer Curve

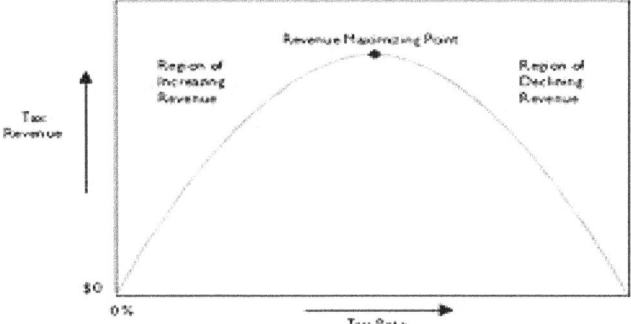

laissez-faire—A French phrase meaning "leave alone." In economics and politics, a doctrine that the economic system functions best when there is no interference by government.

land—An economic resource, along with labor and capital, used to produce goods and services. Includes the original and indestructible powers of the soil and natural resources, such as coal, oil, and metallic ores. There are some important differences. Coal and oil, once they are taken out of the ground and burned, are gone forever. In other words, they are "wasting resources." Fertility of soil does not have to be a wasting resource if the farmer uses farming methods that maintain fertility. But this difference is not absolute. Copper ores, for example, may be used and then recycled.

law of demand—*Ceteris paribus*, if the price of an item falls, then
buyers are willing to buy more of it. Quantity demanded of
a good is inversely related to the good's price.

law of diminishing marginal rate of substitution—The amount of
good A that a consumer is willing to give up in order to get
one additional unit of good B declines as the consumption
of B increases.

law of diminishing marginal utility—As additional units of a
single good are consumed, the marginal utility derived from
the good decreases.

law of diminishing marginal returns—As successive units of a
variable resource are employed (together with a fixed
resource), eventually the marginal product of the variable
resource declines.

law of increasing opportunity cost—As more of a particular good
is produced, larger and larger quantities of an alternative
good must be sacrificed if the economy's resources are
already being used fully and efficiently.

law of supply—Quantity supplied of a good is directly related to
the good's price. If the price of a good rises, suppliers are
willing to supply more of the good.

lazy monopolist—Firm that does not strive for efficiency, but
merely enjoys the position it is already in. (See *X-inefficiency*.)

leading economic indicators—Economic statistics, such as
housing starts. building permits, stock prices, and consumer
expectations that foreshadow future changes in economic
activity.

leakage—Any diversion of aggregate income from the domestic
spending stream; includes saving, taxes, and imports.

learning by doing—Becoming more proficient at doing
something by actually doing it; in the process, learning what
works and what doesn't. Also called on-the-job training.

legal monopoly—The right to be the sole provider of a good or
service, such as a public utility, patent, or copyright.

legal tender—Anything that creditors are required to accept as
payment for debts.

less developed countries—See *developing countries*.

leveraged buy-out—Buying a company using borrowed money to
pay most of the purchase price. The debt is secured against
the assets of the company being acquired. The interest will
be paid out of the company's future cash flow.

liability—Any claim or debt of an individual or business.

LIBOR—Short for London interbank offered rate, the rate of
interest that top-quality banks charge each other for loans.
As a result, it is often used by banks as a base for
calculating the interest rate they charge on other loans.
LIBOR is a floating rate, changing all the time.

limited liability—Owner of the business is liable only to the
extent of his or her own investment.

liquidation—The process of selling all company assets for cash
and using that cash to pay the company's debts; any funds
remaining are distributed to the owners of the business.

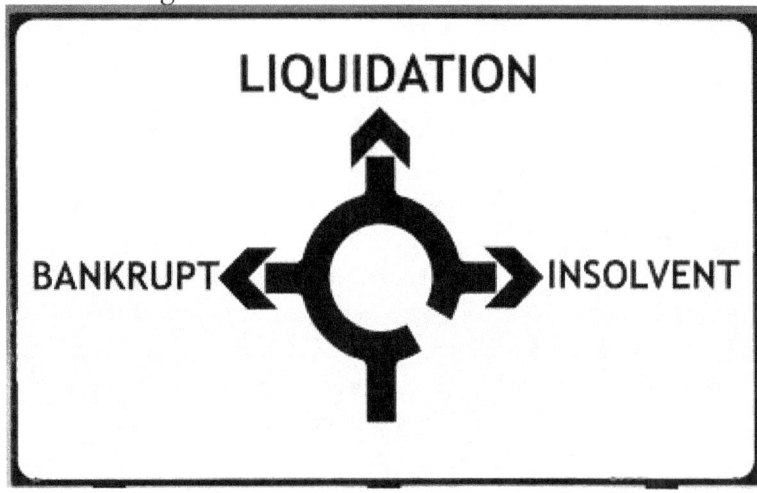

liquidity—How easily an asset can be converted to cash. The ease with which an asset can be converted into cash for an approximation of its true value.

liquidity preference—Proportion of assets individuals and firms choose to hold in varying degrees of liquidity. The more cash they have, the greater is their desire for liquidity.

liquidity ratios—Financial ratios that measure a company's ability to meet its maturing short-term obligations.

Liquidity trap—When monetary policy is impotent. Cutting the rate of interest is supposed to fight recession: raising the money supply increases demand and creates jobs. Keynes argued that sometimes cutting interest, even to zero, may not help. People, banks, and firms could be so risk averse they prefer the liquidity of cash to offering or using credit. In such cases, the economy would be trapped in recession, despite the best efforts of monetary policymakers.

lobbying—Attempting to persuade government officials to make decisions favorable to the lobbyist's cause.

long run—Period of time in which all of a producers resources are variable. (Contrast with *short run*.)

long-run aggregate supply (LRAS) curve—The vertical line drawn at the economy's potential real output.

long-run decision—A decision in which the firm can choose among all possible production techniques. (Contrast with *short-run decision*.)

long-run Phillips curve—A vertical line drawn at the economy's "natural rate of unemployment" that traces equilibrium points that can occur when employers and workers have the time and the ability to adjust fully to any unexpected change in aggregate demand.

long-term assets—In accounting, assets that a company plans to
hold indefinitely or for a long time—generally more than a
year—to generate income. Contrast with short-term assets.

long-term budget—A budget that generally covers periods of
more than one year. Contrast with short-term budget.

Lorenz curve—A geometric representation of the size
distribution of income among families in a given country at
a given time. It shows the inequality of income or wealth in
an economy; the more bowed the curve is from a straight
45-degree diagonal, the greater the inequality. (See Gini
coefficient.)

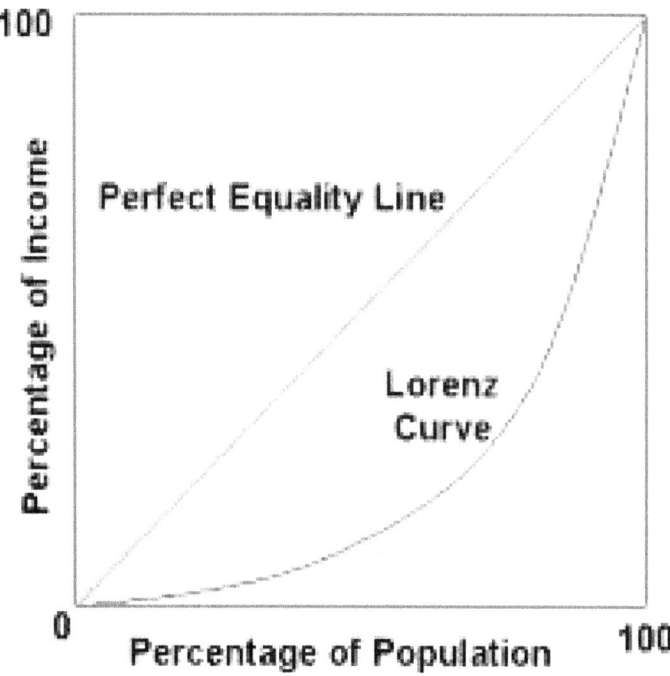

Lorenz Curve for the U.S. 1929, 1970, and 2003

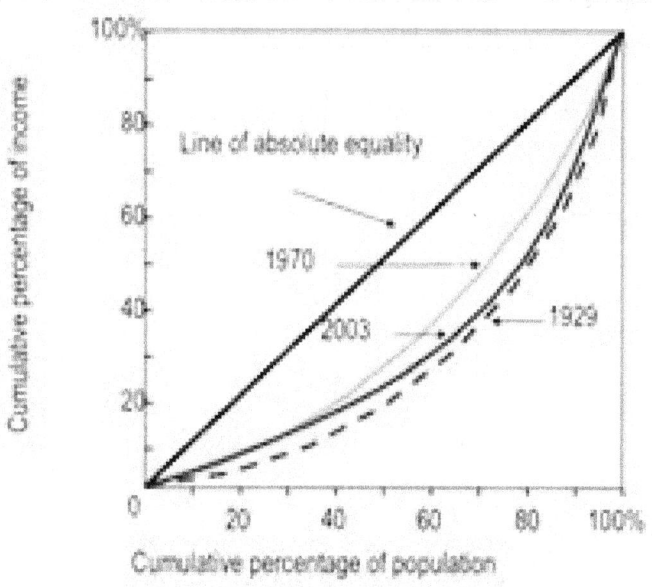

Income equality improved from 1929, the last Republican year before the Great Depression, to 1970, the end of eight Democratic years, and then worsened to 2003, with 23 years of Republican administrations. In short, income disparity grows under Republican administrations and diminishes under Democratic presidents.

lump-sum tax—A tax that is the same amount for everybody, regardless of income or wealth.

❧ M ❦

M1—A measure of money supply consisting of currency held by the nonbank public, checking accounts, and traveler's checks. It is the narrowest definition of money. Exchanging M1 money for goods and services entails no transaction costs; i.e., the individual loses no interest.

M2—A monetary aggregate consisting of M1 plus savings deposits, small certificates of deposit (CDs), and money market mutual funds. Exchanging M2 money for goods and services entails low transaction costs; the individual loses some interest but not much.

M3—A monetary aggregate consisting of M2 plus negotiable certificates of deposit. Exchanging M3 money for goods and services entails transaction costs; i.e., the individual loses more interest than with M2.

macroeconomic externality—Externality that affects the levels of unemployment, inflation, or growth in an economy as a whole. Example: The government cuts expenditures on health with the result that the labor force is less healthy and less effective and the entire economy is less productive.

macroeconomic policy—Top-down policy by government and central banks, usually intended to maximize growth while keeping down inflation and unemployment. The main instruments of macroeconomic policy are changes in the rate of interest and money supply, known as monetary policy, and changes in taxation and public spending, known as fiscal policy.

macroeconomics—The study of the economy as a whole: aggregate national and international economic system, including inflation, unemployment, business cycles, and growth. Special topics include money and banking, international economics, and economic development. (Contrast with *microeconomics*.)

managed float regime—An exchange rate system in which rates for most currencies float, but central banks still intervene to prevent sharp changes.

management by exception (MBE)—A principle stating that managers should be informed about an operational activity only when a result differs by a specified monetary amount or a specified percentage from what was expected.

managerial theories—Views of how management affects the economic system. **Discretionary** theories assume that managers, with no direct stake in the firm, free from strict supervision by owners, make decisions based on personal goals. **Growth-oriented** theories start from the same base but assume the long-term goal of managers is growth of the enterprise. **Bureaucratic** theories assume owners of the firm also control it and seek strategies to reduce risk.

marginal—The difference made by one extra unit of something.

marginal benefit—Added benefits of a decision above the total benefits one has already derived.

marginal cost—Added cost above what one has already incurred. The increase in total cost when one additional unit of output is produced.

marginal factor cost—The additional cost to a firm of hiring another worker.

marginal physical product (MPP)—Additional units of output that hiring an additional worker will bring about.

marginal product—The increase in total product when an additional unit of a resource is employed, other inputs constant.

marginal productivity theory—The theory that factors of production are paid their marginal revenue product (MRP).

marginal propensity to consume (MPC)—The fraction of a dollar by which consumption rises when disposable income rises by $1.

marginal propensity to import (MPI)—The fraction of a change in income that is spent on imported goods and services; change in total spending on imports divided by the change in income that caused it.

marginal propensity to save (MPS)—The fraction of a dollar by which savings rises when disposable income rises by $1.

marginal rate of substitution (MRS)—A measure of how much of one good a consumer would give up to get one more unit of another good while remaining equally satisfied.

marginal rate of transformation (MRT)—The number of units of one good that must be sacrificed in order to increase production of another good.

marginal resource cost (MRC)—The cost of employing an additional unit of a resource.

marginal revenue—The change in a firm's total revenue that occurs when its sales rise by one unit.

marginal revenue curve—Graphical measure of the change in revenue that occurs in response to a change in price.

marginal revenue product (MRP)—The additional revenue made possible by employing an additional unit of a resource. MRP of a worker = Value of the worker's marginal product = Marginal Physical Product (MPP) x Price of Product.

marginal tax rate—Tax rate on an additional dollar of income.

marginal utility—The satisfaction one gets from consuming an additional unit of a product above and beyond what one has consumed up to that point. (Contrast with *total utility*.)

market—A setting in which buyers and sellers establish prices for identical or very similar products, and exchange goods or services.

market capitalization—The market value of a company's shares: the quoted share price multiplied by the total number of shares that the company has issued.

market-clearing price—The price that balances the amount buyers want to buy with the amount sellers want to sell. Also called equilibrium price.

market demand—The sum of all individual demands in a given market at a particular time.

market demand curve—Horizontal sum of all individual demand curves.

market economy—The national economy of a country that relies on market forces to determine levels of production, consumption, investment, and savings without government intervention.

market failure—A condition that arises when unconstrained operation of markets yields socially undesirable results. A completely free market results in too much or too little of a good or service being produced and consumed or failure to achieve efficiency or equity aims of the economy. (See *externalities*.)

market force—An economic force working through the market.

market incentive program—Program that makes the price of a resource reflect a negative externality. An alternative to direct regulation that uses market forces to achieve a desired outcome. Examples: tax incentive program and marketable certificate program.

market niche—A small but profitable segment of a market suitable for focused attention by a marketer.

market period—Period of time too short for sellers to alter their quantity supplied.

market power—When one buyer or seller in a market has the ability to exert significant influence over the quantity of goods and services traded or the price at which they are sold. Market power does not exist when there is perfect competition, but it does when there is a monopoly, monopsony, or oligopoly.

market structure—Physical characteristics of the market within which firms interact. The four market structures are perfect competition, monopolistic competition, oligopoly, and monopoly.

market supply curve—Horizontal sum of all the firms' marginal cost curves, taking account of any changes in input prices that might occur.

market price—The price at which goods or services and money will actually be exchanged. The price corresponding to the point at which supply equals demand.

marketable certificate program—A program that formalizes rights by issuing certificates and allowing trading of those rights.

marketing—The way a business organization identifies its customers, defines and develops the products or services that its customers want, and sells and distributes those products or services to customers.

Marx, Karl—German philosopher, economist, sociologist, historian, journalist, and revolutionary socialist. His ideas played a significant role in the development of social science and the socialist political movement.

Karl Heinrich Marx (1818-1883)

Marxist economists—Those who generally adhere to the principles of Karl Marx and who rely on the dialectical method to investigate the world.

mass consumption—An economy that relies heavily on consumer expenditures.

mass production—The production of goods and services on a large scale, using division of labor and advanced machinery or technology and manufacturing methods.

material balance—In a command economy, process by which central planners adjust incoming and outgoing quantities of materials until supply equals demand. In practice, this process has never worked, largely because economies—even those of small nations—are too large and too complex for any group of individuals to manage.

MC = MR—The profit-maximizing rule. Firms in any market structure maximize their profit (or minimize their loss) when they produce that quantity of output corresponding to the point at which its marginal cost is equal to its marginal revenue.

means-tested transfer payments—Government payments to individuals who must fall below a specified income (and wealth) level to qualify.

medium of exchange—Anything that facilitates trade by being generally accepted by all parties in payment for goods and services.

Menu costs of inflation—Costs to change prices. Just as a restaurant prints a new menu when it changes prices, other firms face costs when they cut or raise prices. Firms may be slow to change prices when there is a shift in the balance of supply and demand, so there will be sticky prices, and the market for their output will be in disequilibrium. Internet may sharply reduce menu costs as it allows prices to be changed at the click of a mouse, improving efficiency.

mercantilism—Economic system in which government doles out the rights to undertake economic activities, opposed by Adam Smith in *Wealth of Nations*. (See *neomercantilism*.)

merger—Combination of two firms.

merit goods or activities—Things government believes are good for you, although you may not think so; e.g., government may subsidize the arts even though you may not like the arts. (Contrast with *demerit goods or activities*.)

microeconomics—The study of markets and how firms and households make decisions about the allocation of their scarce resources. Some special topics include agricultural economics, environmental economics, labor economics, and the economics of poverty. Sometimes called "price theory" in a market economy. (Contrast with *macroeconomics*.)

military-industrial complex—Mutually beneficial relations among armed services, weapons industries, and government officials. Coined by a speechwriter for the farewell address by U.S. President Dwight Eisenhower, who warned against this unhealthy collusion.

minimum level of production—Amount of production run that spreads out set-up costs sufficiently for a firm to undertake production profitably.

minimum wage—The lowest legal wage an employer can pay workers.

Minsky Cycle—A series of Minsky moments in which a period of stability encourages risk taking, which leads to a period of instability, which causes more conservative and risk-averse (de-leveraging) behavior, until stability is restored, continuing the cycle. In this more general view, the Minsky Cycle may apply to a wide range of human activities, beyond investment economics.

Minsky moment—A sudden major collapse of asset values which is part of the credit cycle or business cycle. Formulated by economist Hyman Minsky.

misery index—The sum of a country's inflation and unemployment rates. The higher the score, the greater the economic misery.

MITI—Japanese government agency (Ministry of Industry and Trade) that helps businesses to coordinate policies.

mixed economy—An economic system in which both the government and private enterprise play important roles with regard to production, consumption, investment, and savings. A balance is sought between efficiency and equity. Every economy in the world is a mixed economy.

mobility—Ability of factors of production to move to where they are most valuable. Allows efficient allocation of the world's scarce resources.

model—Framework for looking at the world.

monetarism—A school of thought that fluctuations in economic activity are largely governed by fluctuations in the stock of money. A common belief in this school is that inflation is caused by excess growth in the money supply. This view derives from the "quantity theory of money."

monetary neutrality—Theory that changes in the money supply have no effect on real economic variables such as output, real interest rates, and unemployment. If the central bank doubles the money supply, the price level will double too.

monetary policy—Central bank actions to influence the availability and cost of money and credit as a means of helping to promote low unemployment, stimulate economic growth, stabilize prices, and provide a sustainable pattern of international transactions. Implemented by the Fed.

money—Anything generally accepted as payment for goods, services, resources, and debt. A medium that circulates throughout the economy, facilitating exchange of resources and products among individual economic units. Commodity money, e.g., gold, has intrinsic worth; fiat money, e.g., paper currency, has only the value determined by the market. (See *M1, M2,* and *M3.*)

money market—Market for short-term credit instruments such as Treasury bills with a maturity of less than one year.

money market mutual funds—Mutual funds that use the resources of their investors to buy money market certificates.

money multiplier—The reciprocal of the reserve ratio.

money supply—The amount of money in circulation in the economy. Usually measured by M2.

monitoring costs—Costs incurred by the organizer of production to see that employees do what they are supposed to do.

monitoring problem—Employees' self-interest often differs from the owner's interest, which forces the owner to monitor the employee.

monopolistic competition—A market structure in which many firms sell differentiated products. If one seller raises its prices, its risk of losing sales is less than with an oligopoly.

monopoly—A market with only one seller. The sole seller of a good or service for which there are no good substitutes.

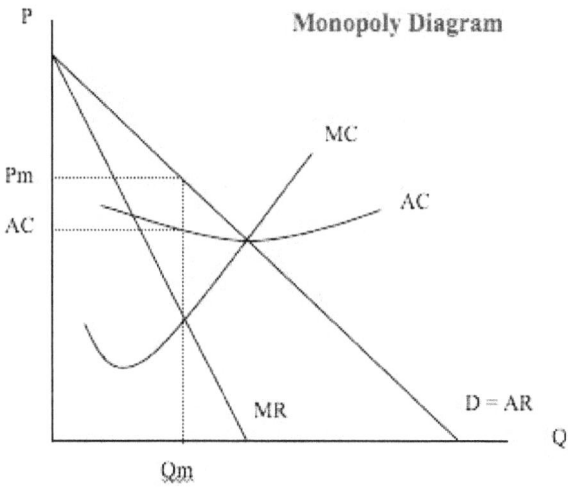

Monopoly Diagram

As with all profit-maximizing firms, the monopolist will produce that quantity at which MC=MR. But that point results in lower quantity and higher price than in a competitive market.

monopoly power—Ability to prevent others from entering a business field, which enables a firm to raise its prices above competitive prices by reducing its output.

monopsony—A market with one buyer, e.g., government is sole buyer of military aircraft. In a small mining town, the single employer is a monopsonist in the town's labor market. NBA, NFL, MLB are single buyers of top athletic talent.

moral hazard—People with insurance may take greater risks than they would without it, as they know they are protected, so the insurer may get more claims than it bargained for.

mortgage—Long-term loan to purchase property.

most favored nation—Country that will pay as low a tariff on its exports as will any other country.

movement along a demand curve—A change in the quantity demanded due to a change in price. (Contrast with *shift factors of demand* and *shift in demand*.)

movement along a supply curve—A change in the quantity supplied due to a change in price.

multinational corporation—A corporation with substantial operations on both the production and sales sides in more than one country.

multiplier—The ratio of a change in equilibrium income to the initial change in expenditure that brought it about. For instance, suppose a government loosens fiscal policy, increasing net public spending by pumping an extra $1 billion into education. This has an immediate effect by increasing the income of teachers and of people who sell educational supplies or build or maintain schools. These people will in turn spend some of their extra money, putting more cash into the pockets of others, who spend some of it, and so on. The multiplier is equal to the reciprocal of the marginal propensity to save (1/MPS). U.S. MPS is 0.05. Therefore the multiplier is 20. The $1billion results in an increase of $20 billion.

mutual fund—An account established by a financial services company that combines the money of many people and invests it in a variety of financial instruments. The company continually offers new shares and buys existing shares back on demand and uses its funds to buy a diversified group of securities of other companies. Money is collected from individuals and invested on their behalf in varied portfolios of stocks, bonds, and other financial instruments.

❧ N ❧

NAFTA—North American Free Trade Agreement, a regional trade agreement that took effect in 1994, aimed at reducing and eliminating tariffs between its three members: Canada, Mexico, and the United States.

NAIRU—The non-accelerating-inflation rate of unemployment. Preferred over "natural unemployment rate."

Nash equilibrium—A situation in which economic actors interacting with one another each choose their best strategy given the strategies that all the other actors have chosen. Named for Nobel Laureate John Nash.

National Association of Securities Dealers Automated Quotation System (NASDAQ)—An automated information network that provides brokers and dealers with price quotations on some 5,000 active securities traded "over-the-counter," i.e., not on a trading floor, where the "open outcry" auction system was commonly used until recently.

national bank—A commercial bank that operates under a charter granted by a federal regulatory agency and is subject to regulation and supervision by federal regulators.

National Bank of Georgia—The central bank of the Republic of Georgia. (Not to be confused with *Bank of Georgia*, a private bank.)

national debt—Total amount of debt that government owes to the public; equals the sum of all past budget deficits, minus past budget surpluses.

national income (NI)—Aggregate income earned by households for use of their resources in production. Net national product plus government subsidies minus indirect business taxes.

nationalization—The act by government of taking over and providing services previously owned and operated by private sector enterprise. (Contrast with *privatization*.)

natural monopoly—Monopoly that exists because economies of scale create a barrier to entry. Examples are public utilities, firms with patents, and chicken and hog producers. *Excludable* but not *rival.*

natural rate hypothesis—The natural rate of unemployment is largely independent of the stimulus provided by monetary or fiscal policy.

natural rate of unemployment—Combination of frictional and structural unemployment that persists in an efficient, expanding economy when labor and resource markets are in equilibrium. Modern economists reject the term and prefer NAIRU or long-term unemployment, as there is nothing *natural* about unemployment.

natural resources—Unaltered gifts of nature. One of the factors of production sometimes called "land."

near moneys—Financial assets that are like money but that do not serve as mediums of exchange. Example: short-dated securities with a government guarantee that are either marketable or redeemable by government at short notice.

negative income tax—A way of building redistribution into the taxation system by taking money from people with high incomes and paying it to people with low incomes. Because it takes place automatically through the tax system, it may attach less stigma to the receipt of financial help than some other forms of welfare assistance.

neoclassical economics—Approach that analyzes how individuals and firms should behave to maximize their own objective functions, assuming activities are coordinated by the price mechanism, and that markets clear so that the economy is in equilibrium at all times. Criticisms of neoclassical economics relate mainly to the excessive simplicity of the initial assumptions and to the impractical complexity of the derived implications for business decisions.

neomercantilism—Market economy guided by government that prefers an export-driven economy, e.g., Japan and China.

net assets—The difference between the value of a firm's total assets and its total liabilities.

net domestic product (NDP)—GDP minus depreciation; a measure of the value of aggregate output produced in a country and available for use.

net exports $(X - M)$—Exports of goods and services (X) minus imports of goods and services (M). When this number is positive it is known as a trade surplus; when it is negative it is a trade deficit.

net income—For a business organization, any money that remains from the company's sales revenues after deductions have been made for sales costs, operating expenses, and taxes. Also known as profit, profit margin, and spread. Contrast with net loss.

net investment—Gross investment minus depreciation. The amount by which the capital stock is increased during a period.

net loss—For a business organization, the amount of a company's expenses (sales costs, operating expenses, and taxes) for a reporting period that exceeds its revenues for the period. Contrast with net income.

net national product (NNP)—GNP minus depreciation; a measure of the value of aggregate output available for use.

net present value (NPV)—A measure used to help decide whether or not to proceed with an investment. Both the costs and benefits of the investment are included.

net taxes (NT)—Taxes minus transfer payments (e.g., social security).

net unilateral transfers—The unilateral transfers (gifts and grants) received from abroad by residents of a country minus the unilateral transfers these residents send to foreign residents.

net wealth—The value of a household's assets minus its liabilities.

net worth—In accounting, the difference between a person's or an organization's assets and liabilities.

network effect—When the value of a good to a consumer changes because the number of people using it changes. For instance, owning a phone becomes more valuable as more people are plugged into the telephone network.

neural network—A computer system modeled on the human brain and nervous system.

New Deal—U.S. economic reform programs of the 1930s established to help lift the country out of the Great Depression.

New York Stock Exchange—The world's largest exchange for trading stocks and bonds.

NGO—Non-government organization.

NIMBY—"Not In My Back Yard," said by people who approve of a project but do not want it to be built near them.

nirvana criticism—Comparing reality to a situation that cannot occur.

Nominal GDP—The production of goods and services valued at current prices (not adjusted for inflation).

nominal interest rate—A rate quoted contractually by a lender or a borrower and does not take into account the effects of compounding. The nominal interest rate will always be less than the effective interest rate. Also known as stated interest rate. Contrast with effective interest rate.

nominal value—Value measured in current-year dollars, i.e., not adjusted for inflation.

nominal wage—The wage measured in terms of current dollars, i.e., not adjusted for inflation; the dollars received in the pay envelope or directly deposited in the earner's bank account.

nonactivists—Those who consider the private sector to be relatively stable and able to absorb economic shocks without discretionary government policy.

nonconvertible currency—A currency that cannot be freely exchanged with currencies of other nations; includes the currencies of most of the world's nations.

nonprice competition—Trying to win business from rivals other than by charging a lower price. Methods include advertising, slightly differentiating your product, improving its quality, or offering free gifts or discounts on subsequent purchases.

nonsufficient funds (NSF) checks—Checks that cannot be honored by the issuing financial institution because the checking account holder did not have enough money in his or her checking account to pay the amount of the check.

nontariff barrier—Government measures, such as imports monitoring systems and variable levies, other than tariffs, that have the effect of restricting imports or that have the potential for restricting international trade.

normal good—A good whose demand rises when buyers' incomes rise. Most goods are normal goods.

normal profits—Returns to business owners for the opportunity cost of their implicit inputs. Amounts that an entrepreneur could get by supplying entrepreneurship to the market.

normative criticism—The desirability of a Pareto optimal position depends on the desirability of the starting position. If one objects to the starting position, one will also likely object to the Pareto optimal position.

normative economics—Study of how an economy should be from society's standpoint.

normative economic statement—A statement that represents an opinion, which cannot be proved or disproved.

notes payable—Short-term loans owed by the firm.

৯৯ O ৶

objective—(1) Keeping one's personal views or value judgments out of an analysis. (2) A goal or aim to be achieved.

OECD—Organization for Economic Cooperation and Development, a Paris-based club for industrialized countries and the best of the rest.

Office of the Comptroller of the Currency (OCC)—A bureau of the U.S. Department of the Treasury responsible for regulating national banks.

official transactions account—That part of the U.S. balance of payments account that records the amount of dollars a nation buys.

offshore—Where the usual rules of a person's or firm's home country do not apply.

Okun's law—A description of what happens to unemployment when the rate of growth of GDP changes, based on empirical research by Arthur Okun (1928-80). It predicts that if GDP grows at 3% a year, the unemployment rate will be unchanged. If it grows faster, the unemployment rate will fall by half of what the growth rate exceeds 3% by; that is, if GDP grows by 5%, unemployment will fall by 1 percentage point. Likewise, a lesser, say 2%, increase in GDP would be associated with a half a percentage point increase in the unemployment rate.

oligopoly—A market with a few interdependent sellers, e.g., cars. Without cooperation (illegal price-fixing), if one seller raises its prices, it risks losing all or much of its sales.

oligopsony—A market in which there are very few buyers; e.g., McDonald's, Burger King, and Wendy's control much of the U.S. meat market.

OPEC—The Organization of Petroleum Exporting Countries, a CARTEL set up in 1960 to control crude oil output by member countries, thereby maintaining high prices.

109

open corporation—One whose stock is sold to the public.
open market operations—Buying and selling of previously owned
   government securities by the central bank in the secondary
   financial market.
open shop—A firm in which members may choose whether or
   not to join a union. (Contrast with *closed shop* and *union shop*.)
open trading system—A trading system in which countries allow
   fair and nondiscriminatory access to each other's markets.
operational budget—A budget that includes part or all of a
   company's core business operations.
operational planning—The company process of determining how
   to accomplish specified tasks with available resources, given
   a company's strategic plan.
opportunity cost—Value of the next best alternative surrendered
   when a choice is made. The benefit you give up when you
   don't choose a particular activity because you have decided
   to choose a different activity.

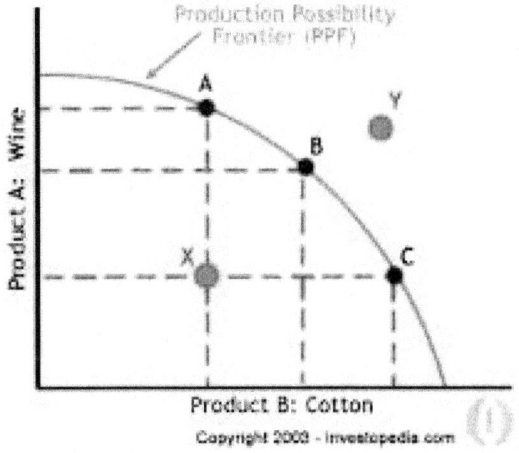

The Production Possibility Frontier demonstrates the
concept of opportunity cost. To get more of one thing, we
must give up some of another thing.

optimal level of pollution—Amount of pollution at which the marginal benefit of reducing pollution equals the marginal cost.

optimal policy—Policy whose marginal cost equals its marginal benefit.

optimum—As good as it gets, given the constraints. For the concept of optimum to mean anything, there must be both a goal, say, to maximize economic productivity, and a set of constraints, such as a set of scarce resources. Optimizing is the process of doing the best you can in the circumstances.

output—The result of an activity.

output gap—How far an economy's current output is below what it would be at full capacity.

outsourcing—Shifting activities that used to be done inside a firm to an outside company, which can do them more cost-effectively. This is a "make-buy" decision for the firm.

overheating—When an economy is growing too fast and its productive capacity cannot keep up with *demand*. It often boils over into *inflation*.

over-the counter—Figurative term for the means of trading securities that are not listed on an organized stock exchange such as the American or New York Stock Exchanges.

over-the-counter (OTC) market—A way of trading securities in which dealers at different locations who have an inventory of securities stand ready to buy and sell securities through a telecommunications network that brings the buyers and sellers together. NASDAQ is the most widely used OTC market in the United States. (See *National Association of Securities Dealers Automated Quotation System*.)

overhead costs—Fixed costs of doing business, such as executive salaries, interest payments on loans, and facilities rent.

৯ P ৎ

panic—A series of unexpected cash withdrawals from a bank caused by a sudden decline in depositor confidence or fear that the bank will be closed by the chartering agency; i.e., many depositors withdraw cash almost simultaneously. Since the cash reserve a bank keeps on hand is only a small fraction of its deposits, a large number of withdrawals in a short period of time can deplete available cash and force the bank to close and possibly go out of business.

paradox of thrift—Attempts by households to save a larger percentage of their disposable income may not increase the total dollar amount of aggregate personal savings. This is caused by a decline in consumption, which results in lower national income and, therefore, less national savings rather than more.

Pareto optimal criterion—The concept that no person can be made better off without another being made worse off. Named for Italian economist Wilfredo Pareto (1843–1923).

Pareto optimal policies—Policies that benefit some people but hurt no one.

partnership—A business owned by two or more people not incorporated, with each partner liable for the actions of all other partners.

par value of stock—The designated legal value assigned to each outstanding share of common stock; primarily used for accounting purposes. Also known as nominal value and face value.

parity price—In agricultural economics, a price that maintains the ratio of prices received by farmers and prices paid by farmers to a base year.

parity ratio—Prices received by farmers for their output divided by prices paid by farmers for their inputs.

partial equilibrium analysis—Analysis that assumes all other thing remain equal. (Contrast with *general equilibrium analysis*.)

partially flexible exchange rate—The government sometimes affects the exchange rate and sometimes leaves it to the market.

patent—A legal monopoly granted to an inventor of a new product or process exclusivity for a period of time. Creates a barrier to entry by other firms.

payback period—In capital budgeting, the number of years that must pass before the earnings a product produces equal the initial investment in the product.

peak—The top of the business cycle between expansion and downturn. A time when firms are producing at or near capacity and unemployment is low.

pension—A lifetime monthly income benefit payable to a person upon his or her retirement.

pension funds—Retirement accounts that people obtain through their employers while they are working.

per capita—Per person.

perestroika—The restructuring of what had been the Soviet economy to promote more decentralization, less bureaucracy, and greater individual incentives; the name of a book by Mikhail Gorbachev outlining these initiatives.

perfect competition—A market in which there are (theoretically) an infinite number of sellers, perfectly homogeneous products, perfect information, and no barriers to entry or departure. All sellers are price takers. As in all market structures, a profit-maximizing firm in a perfectly competitive market will produce that output corresponding to the point at which its marginal cost is equal to its marginal revenue.

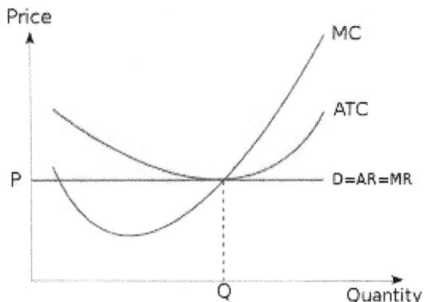

The profit maximizing firm will produce quantity Q.

perfectly elastic—A condition in which infinitesimally small changes in price cause infinitely large changes in quantity. In other words, quantity is hyper, super, infinitely responsive to price. Any change in price, no matter how small triggers an infinite change in quantity. (Contrast with *perfectly inelastic, relatively elastic, relatively inelastic,* and *unit elastic.*)

perfectly inelastic—A condition in which changes in price do NOT cause any change in quantity. In other words, quantity is totally, completely unresponsive to price. Quantity just does not change, regardless of changes in price. (Contrast with *perfectly elastic, relatively elastic, relatively inelastic,* and *unit elastic.*)

personal income—The amount of before-tax income received by households. National income less income earned but not received plus income received but not earned.

perverse incentive—Incentive to use goods in a manner that does not reflect that use's cost to society. This happens when government intervenes in a market, setting a price that differs from the free market equilibrium price. Example: Government decides to impose a price ceiling on a good; then people will find other, less efficient, uses for that good.

petrodollar—U.S. dollar earned from the sale of oil, or oil revenues denominated in U.S. dollars.

Phillips curve—A curve showing possible combinations of the inflation rate, given the expected price level.

picketing—Efforts by unions to inform the public of a labor dispute by parading in front of their workplace with signs displaying their grievances.

Pigou effect—Named after Arthur Pigou (1877-1959), a sort of wealth effect resulting from *deflation*. A fall in the price level increases the real value of people's *savings*, making them feel wealthier and thus causing them to spend more. This increase in *demand* can lead to higher *employment*.

pillars of free enterprise—Private property, the price system, market competition, and entrepreneurship.

planned investment—The amount of investment firms plan to undertake during a year.

pleonexia—A concept that roughly corresponds to extreme greed, covetousness, or avarice, and is strictly defined as "the insatiable desire to have what rightfully belongs to others," suggesting what John W. Ritenbaugh describes as "ruthless self-seeking and an arrogant assumption that others and things exist for one's own benefit."

positive economic statement—A statement that can be proved or disproved by reference to facts.

positive economics—The study of what is, and how the economy works.

positive vs. normative economics—A **positive** statement is a statement about **what is** and contains no approval or disapproval. A positive statement can be wrong. "The moon is made of green cheese" is incorrect, but it is a positive statement because it is a statement about what exists. A **normative** statement expresses judgment about whether a situation is desirable or not. "The world would be a better place if the moon were made of green cheese" is a normative statement because it expresses a judgment about **what ought to be**. There is no way of disproving this statement. If you disagree with it, you have no sure way of convincing someone who believes the statement that he is wrong.

potential output—The economy's maximum sustainable output level, given the supply of resources, the state of technology, and the underlying economic institutions.

poverty—Defined by the U.S. government as less than three times an average family's minimum food expenditures as calculated by the U.S. Department of Agriculture.

predatory pricing—Charging low prices now so you can charge much higher prices later. The predator charges so little that it may sustain losses over a period of time, in the hope that its rivals will be driven out of business.

preferred stock—A share in the ownership of a corporation that offers first rights to any dividends or a share of the assets if the corporation is liquidated.

premium—The price one pays for insurance.

present value (PV)—The amount of money that must be invested today in order to accumulate a specified amount of money by a certain date. Contrast with future value (FV).

price—The mechanism that allocates scarce resources in a market economy. In equilibrium, price balances supply and demand. The price charged for something depends on the tastes, income, and relative prices of substitutes and complements of customers. It depends on the amount of competition in the market.

price ceiling—A legal maximum amount that sellers are permitted to charge for a good or service.

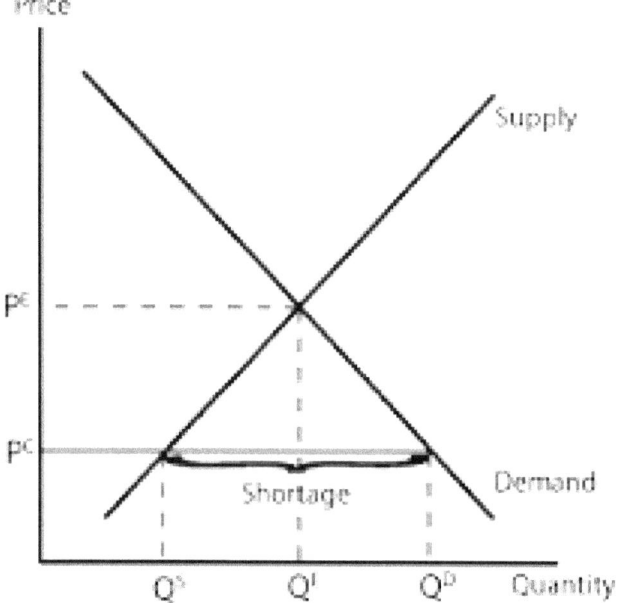

A binding price ceiling, fixed below the equilibrium price

price discrimination—Actions by sellers that give certain buyers advantages over buyers. The practice of selling the same product for less to one buyer than to another.

price effect—People buy less of something at higher prices than they do at lower prices. (See *law of demand*.)

price elasticity of demand—Percentage change in quantity demanded, divided by percentage change in price. (Contrast with *income elasticity of demand*.)

price elasticity of demand—The relative response of a change in quantity demanded to a relative change in price. More specifically, the price elasticity of demand can be defined as the percentage change in quantity demanded due to a percentage change in demand price. (Contrast with *price elasticity of supply*.)

price elasticity of supply—The relative response of a change in quantity supplied to a relative change in price. More specifically, the price elasticity of supply can be defined as the percentage change in quantity supplied due to a percentage change in supply price. (Contrast with *price elasticity of demand*.)

price fixing—Actions, generally by several large corporations that dominate in a single market, to escape market discipline by setting prices for goods and services at an agreed-on level.

price floor—A legal minimum price that sellers may receive for a good or service.

price index—A measure of the average price level of a basket of goods.

price leadership—A form of oligopoly in which the dominant firm sets prices, and the smaller firms follow its pricing policy.

price level—A composite measure reflecting the prices of all goods and services in the economy.

price stabilization program—In agricultural economics, a program designed to reduce or eliminate short-run fluctuations in prices received by farmers and allow prices to follow their long-term trend line.

price stability—The absence of inflation or deflation; a period of time during which there is little change in what the currency can buy.

price support program—In agricultural economics, a government program that maintains prices at a higher level than the market trend of prices.

price supports—Government assistance provided to farmers to help them deal with such unfavorable factors as bad weather and overproduction.

price system—The use of prices to allocate scarce resources. As people make exchanges, markets establish prices for goods, services, and resources.

price taker—A firm or individual who takes the market price as given.

primary market—New issues market where investment bankers sell new shares of stocks and new bonds.

principal (1)—One for whom another, the agent, performs an act.

principal (2)—The amount of money borrowed.

principle of increasing marginal opportunity cost—Initial opportunity costs are low but they increase the more you concentrate on the activity. (See *opportunity cost.*)

private good—A good that is *excludable* and *rivalrous*. Only those who pay can use the good, and when consumed by one individual, cannot be consumed by other individuals; e.g., an M&M candy or an airplane seat in flight.

private property—Capital and other resources owned by individuals or firms rather than government.

private property rights—Exclusive control of an asset or a right by a private individual or firm.

privatization—The act of turning previously government-provided services over to private sector enterprise. (Contrast with *nationalization*.)

probability—A likelihood that a particular outcome will occur. A probability of zero means the outcome is impossible. A probability of 1 means the particular outcome is a certainty. A probability of 0.5 means the particular outcome of interest may or may not occur with equal likelihood.

producer surplus—The difference between the price at which producers would have been willing to supply a good and the price they actually receive. The excess of total sales revenue going to producers over the area under the supply curve for a good. If the supply curve is perfectly elastic, there is no producer surplus.

product—A good or a service. A good is a tangible product, e.g., automobile or a bushel of corn. A service is an intangible product, e.g., a haircut or bus ride.

product differentiation—Process of creating uniqueness in a product.

product market—A market in which goods and services are exchanged.

product mix—The total assortment of products offered by a company.

production—A process of creating or increasing the capacity for creating goods and services to satisfy human desires. It is measured in units of output per unit of input.

production function—Equation that describes the relationships between inputs and outputs, telling the maximum amount of output that can be derived from a given number of inputs.

production possibilities—The possible combination of total
   output that could be produced if a nation's resources were
   fully employed.
production possibilities frontier (PPF)—A graph illustrating the
   maximum possible output combinations of an economy
   with a given number of inputs. Illustrates the concept of
   opportunity cost. (See *opportunity cost*.)

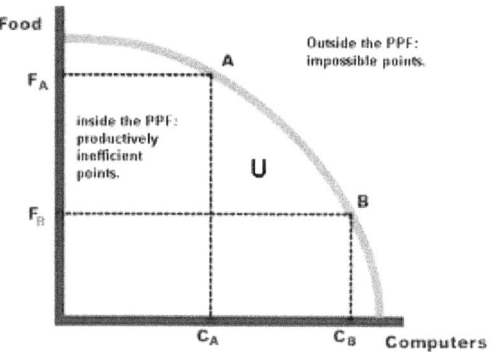

Production possibilities frontier

production table—A table showing output that will result from
   various combinations of factors of production or inputs.
productive efficiency—Getting as much output for as few inputs
   as possible.
productivity—The ratio of output of goods and services
   produced per unit of input of productive resources over
   some period of time. In general, a nation becomes wealthier
   as it becomes more productive. Some ways in which a
   nation may become more productive include the following:
   increase in quantities of resources available; discovery of
   new technologies; increases in the division of labor and
   specialization; improvements in the allocation of existing
   resources; and increases in the rate of use of existing
   resources.

profit—Payments received by businesses from selling goods and
services minus the costs incurred by those businesses.
(Revenue less costs.)

profit margin—Difference between cost and selling price.

profit-maximizing rule #1—A firm will maximize profits (or
minimize losses) by producing the quantity of total product
at which marginal cost equals marginal revenue: **MC=MR**

profit-maximizing rule #2—A firm maximizes profits by
employing units of a resource where its marginal revenue
product equals its marginal resource cost.

profit motive—The desire to benefit from the investment of time
and money in a business enterprise.

progressive tax—One that takes a larger percentage of a higher
income and a smaller percentage of a lower income.
Average tax rate increases with income. (Contrast with
regressive tax.)

proletariat—The working class, e.g., laborers, blue collar
employees, and low-level office workers.

Poster representing the proletariat

Propensity—May apply to consumption, saving, investment, import, etc. The *average* propensity to consume (APC) is total consumption divided by total income. The *marginal* propensity to consume (MPC) measures how much of each extra dollar of income is consumed: the percentage change in consumption divided by the percentage change in income.

property rights—The rights to use or dispose of specified property as one sees fit.

proportional income tax—Takes the same percentage of a higher income as of a lower income. Average tax rate is constant with income. (Contrast with *progressive tax* and *regressive tax*.)

protectionism—The deliberate use of restrictions on imports to enable relatively inefficient domestic producers to compete successfully with more efficient foreign producers. Also called economic nationalism.

proven reserves—Resource reserves that have been discovered and documented to date.

public assistance—Also called "welfare." Means-tested social programs targeted to the poor and providing financial, nutritional, medical, and housing assistance.

public choice economists—Economists who integrate an economic analysis of politics with their analysis of the economy.

public good—Good whose consumption by one individual does not prevent its consumption by other individuals. It is available to all to consume, regardless of who pays and who does not. Not *excludable* and not *rivalrous*. Example: A defense force.

public-private—Using private firms to carry out aspects of government.

public saving—The tax revenue that the government has left over after paying for its spending. A budget surplus.

public spending—Spending by national and local government and some government-backed institutions.

public utility—A firm providing essential services to the public, such as water, electricity, and postal services, usually involving elements of natural monopoly and regulated by a public utility commission.

publicly traded securities—Financial instruments, e.g., stocks and bonds, that are bought and sold by the public in securities markets such as stock exchanges and bond markets.

purchasing power parity (PPP)—Method of comparing income by looking at the domestic purchasing power of money in different countries. A method for calculating the correct value of a currency, which may differ from its current market value. It is helpful when comparing living standards in different countries, as it indicates the appropriate exchange rate to use when expressing incomes and prices in different countries in a common currency. By correct value, economists mean the exchange rate that would bring demand and supply of a currency into equilibrium over the long-term.

❧ Q ❧

quantity demanded—Quantity of a good that buyers want to buy at a given price. It can be represented by a point on a demand curve.

quantity supplied—Quantity of a good that suppliers want to sell at a given price. It can be represented by a point on a supply curve.

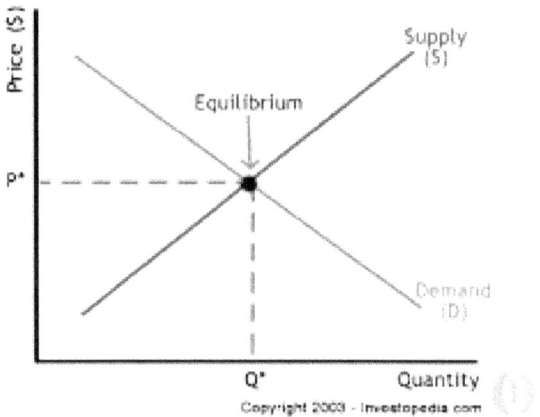

Supply and Demand Graph

quantity theory of money—The theory that the velocity of money is predictable, so changes in the money supply have predictable effects on nominal income. See *monetarism*.

quasi rent—Any payment to a resource above the amount that the resource would receive in its next-best use. Also called producer surplus.

quick ratio—One way of determining a company's ability to liquidate debt immediately, this ratio is calculated by dividing a company's most liquid current assets by the company's current liabilities. Also known as acid-test ratio.

quotas—Quantity limits on imports or exports.

❧ R ❧

Rahn curve—A theory by Richard Rahn proposing a level of
government spending that maximizes economic growth.
The theory is used by classical economists to argue for a
decrease in overall government spending and taxation. The
curve suggests the optimal level of government spending is
15–25% of GDP.

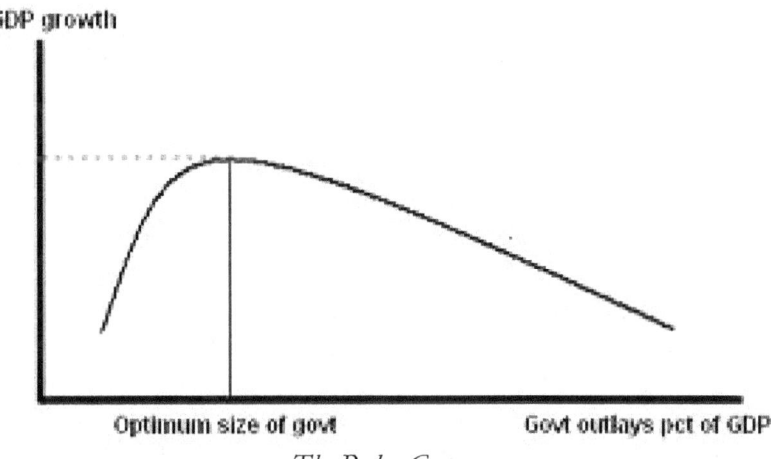

The Rahn Curve

random walk—The path of a variable whose changes are
impossible to predict.
rate of return—Investment earnings expressed as a percentage
relative to the invested principal.
ratings—A guide to riskiness of a financial instrument provided
by a ratings agency, such as Moody's, Standard and Poor's,
and Fitch. These measures of credit quality are mostly
offered on marketable government and corporate debt.
rational choice, principle of—Spend your money on those goods
that give you the most marginal utility per dollar.

rational expectations—A school of thought that claims people form expectations based on all available information, including the probable future actions of government policy makers.

rationing—An alternative to letting prices determine how scarce economic resources, goods, and services are distributed. Non-price rationing is often used when the distribution decided by market forces is perceived to be unfair. Rationing may lead to the creation of a black market, as people sell their rations to those willing to pay a high price

Raupp's rule of capital flow—(1) Capital loves low labor rates. (2) Capital flees from uncertainty and instability.

Rawls maximin—Philosophy of equity, stating that society should maximize the utility of its poorest person.

Reaganomics—The discredited policy of Ronald Reagan based on greed and favoring the rich. Also called "trickle-down economics": the more the rich have, the more will trickle down to the rest of the population. Called "voodoo economics" by George H. W. Bush. It took the United States 200 years to acquire a national debt of one trillion dollars; Reaganomics tripled the debt in just eight years.

real dollars—Nominal dollars adjusted for inflation.

real exchange rate—An exchange rate that has been adjusted to take account of any difference in the rate of inflation in the two countries whose currency is being exchanged.

real GDP—The value of GDP measured in terms of dollars of purchasing power; nominal GDP adjusted for inflation.

real interest rate—Nominal interest rate minus the inflation rate.

real terms—A measure of the value of money that removes the effect of *inflation*. (Contrast with *nominal* value.)

real wage—The wage measured in terms of constant purchasing power, i.e., in terms of the quantity of goods and services it will purchase.

real-world competition—A fight between the forces of
monopolization and the forces of competition.

realization principle—An accounting concept which states that a
company should recognize revenue when it is earned,
regardless of when the company receives the actual
payment, so long as a legal and reasonable expectation
exists that the customer will remit payment in full.

recession—A significant decline in general economic activity
extending over a period of time, usually two consecutive
quarters of negative economic growth.

reciprocity—Doing as you are done by. A grants B certain
privileges on the condition that B grants the same privileges
to A. Most international economic agreements, for
example, on trade, include binding reciprocity requirements.

recognition lag—The time needed to identify a macroeconomic
problem and assess its seriousness.

redlining—Not lending to people in certain poor or troubled
neighborhoods, drawn with a red line on a map, simply
because they live there, regardless of their credit-worthiness
but judged by other criteria, e.g., race or religion.

regional economic integration—A hierarchy of arrangements
extending from preferential tariff agreement to free trade
area, customs union, common market, and, in the extreme
case, economic union. The latter is now frequently
described as economic and monetary union.

regressive tax—One that takes a larger percentage of a lower
income and a smaller percentage of a higher income.
Average tax rate decreases with income. (Contrast with
progressive tax and *proportional tax*.)

regulation—The formulation and issuance by authorized agencies
of specific rules or regulations, under governing law, for the
conduct and structure of a certain industry or activity.

regulatory arbitrage—Exploiting loopholes in regulation, and perhaps making the regulation useless in the process. This is often done by international investors who use derivatives to find ways around a country's financial regulations.

regulatory failure—When regulation generates more economic costs than benefits.

regulatory risk—A risk faced by private-sector firms that regulatory changes will hurt their business. In competitive markets, regulatory risk is usually small. But in natural monopoly industries, such as electricity distribution, it may be huge. To ensure that regulatory risk does not deter private firms from offering their services, a government wishing to change its regulations may have good reason to compensate private firms that suffer losses as a result of the change.

regulatory trade restrictions—Government-imposed procedural rules that limit imports.

relative price—Price of a good compared to the price of some other good.

reliability—In product evaluation, the ability of the good to continue to perform in accordance with its specifications for at least a certain period of time, i.e., quality over time. In accounting, the quality of accounting information that requires a company's accounting records and financial statements to present accurate, objective information that is free from bias and misrepresentation.

rent—(1) Price paid to one who provides the factor of production "land." (2) Income earned when supply is restricted; for example, when a firm persuades government to impose a high tariff on imports of products that compete with its products, the resulting higher prices for its own products are considered *rent*.

rent seeking—Attempting to influence the structure of economic institutions in order to create rents for itself. Firms that lobby legislators engage in rent seeking behavior.

rent seeking loss from monopoly—Waste caused by people spending money trying to get government to give them a monopoly. Example: lobbying.

replacement cost—What it would cost today to replace a firm's existing assets.

replacement rate—The fertility rate required in a country to keep its population steady. In rich countries, this is usually reckoned to be 2.1 children per woman, the extra 0.1 reflecting the likelihood that some children will die before their parents. The U.S. rate in 2015 was 1.87. In poorer countries with higher infant mortality, the rate is higher.

required reserve ratio—Legal minimum ratio of reserves to deposits. The proportion of a bank's deposits that must be kept on reserve in the central bank or in its own vault and not permitted to be used for loans.

required reserves—That portion of a bank's deposits that cannot be loaned.

reserve currency—A currency that countries hold reserves, liquid financial assets with which they can settle debts).

reserves—Funds that banks use to satisfy the cash demands of their customers. Reserves consist of deposits at the central bank plus currency that is physically held by banks.

resource market—A market in which resources are exchanged.

resources—Inputs, or factors of production, including: (1) Land: Gifts of nature used in the production process; (2) Labor: Human talents used in the production process; and (3) Capital: Manufactured things that make other things. Generally, the market economy can grow larger if any of the resources available to it become more plentiful. In other words, we can produce more outputs if we use more inputs.

retained earnings—Undistributed profits; profits (less taxes) reinvested in the business for purchase of new capital resources or to finance other activities without relying on external financing such as new issues of bonds or stock.

revenue—Payments received by businesses from selling goods and services, or payments received by governments from taxes and other sources.

revenue tariff—A tax levied on imports to raise money for the government.

reverse engineering—Dismantling a product in order to gain information about its makeup.

"right-to-work" laws—Anti-union state laws that theoretically guarantee individuals the right to hold a job without being required to join a union but are actually intended to weaken and destroy labor unions. Part of the aggressively hostile anti-union Taft-Hartley Act of 1947 that was passed over President Truman's veto by a conservative Congress.

risk-return tradeoff—An investment principle stating that the interplay between investment risk and return usually results in higher risks offering potentially higher returns, and lower risks offering potentially lower returns.

rival good—A good whose consumption by one consumer prevents simultaneous consumption by other consumers.

Rostow's Stages of Growth model, also called "Rostovian take-off model"—One of the major historical models of economic growth, developed by W. W. Rostow. The model postulates that economic growth occurs in five stages, of varying length:
1. Traditional society,
2. Preconditions for take-off,
3. Take-off,
4. Drive to maturity,
5. Age of high mass consumption.

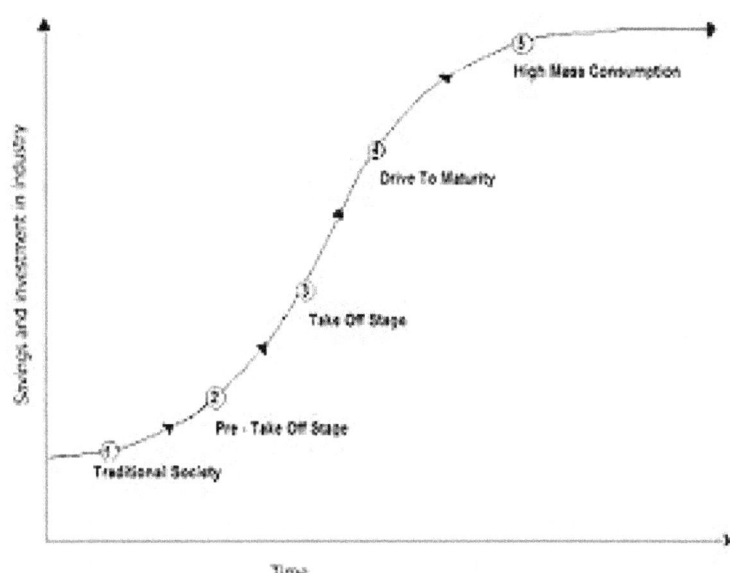

Rostovian take-off model

rule of 70—A certain amount of money will double in value in the number of years obtained when one divides 70 by the interest rate. (Mathematically, the number is closer to 72!) The rule of 70 may be used to estimate how long it would take a country's real GDP to double. For example, if the growth rate of China is 10 percent, the rule of 70 predicts it would take seven years, or 70/10, for China's real GDP to double.

run on assets—A situation in which many customers demand to withdraw their funds from a financial institution at once. The most notable run in U.S. history was at the start of the Great Depression, when bank customers demanded their cash from banks in great numbers. President Roosevelt declared a "bank holiday" to stop the panic.

❧ S ❧

S-corporation—A firm, for United States federal income tax purposes, that is a closely held corporation (or, in some cases, a limited liability company or a partnership) that makes a valid election to be taxed under Subchapter S of Chapter 1 of the Internal Revenue Code. S-corporations do not pay any federal income taxes. Instead, the corporation's income or losses are divided among and passed through to its shareholders. The shareholders must then report the income or loss on their own individual income tax returns.

safe harbor—Protection from the rough seas of regulation. Laws and regulations often include a safe harbor clause that sets out the circumstances in which otherwise regulated firms or individuals can do something without regulatory oversight or interference.

salary—Earnings of employees paid on a weekly or monthly basis rather than hourly.

sales revenue—The total dollar value of sales volume.

sales tax—A regressive tax added to the price of goods when they are sold.

sales volume—The number of units of product sold.

satisficing—Settling for what is good enough, rather than the best that is possible. Coined by Nobel Laureate Herbert Simon.

saving function—The relation between saving and level of income in the economy, other things constant.

savings—Any income that is not spent. Ultimately, savings are the source of investment in an economy, although domestic savings may be supplemented by capital from foreign savers or themselves be invested abroad. Savings include purchases of shares or other financial securities, as well as deposits in savings accounts, checking accounts, and certificates of deposit (CDs).

savings and loan association (S&L)—A depository institution that gets the majority of its deposits from consumers and makes the majority of its loans as home mortgage loans. Also known as savings bank and thrift. Reckless removal of safeguards by the Reagan and Bush administrations in the 1980s caused a virtual collapse of the S&L industry in the U.S., costing taxpayers hundreds of billions of dollars to protect depositors.

savings deposits—Deposits that earn interest but have no maturity date.

Say's Law—supply creates its own demand. So argued French economist, Jean-Baptiste Say (1767-1832), and many classical and neo-classical economists since. Keynes argued against Say, making the case for the use of fiscal policy to boost demand if there is not enough of it to produce full employment.

scab—One who crosses a picket line to take the place of a striking worker.

scalability—The ease with which the supply of an economic product or process can be expanded to meet increased demand.

scarce—The amount people desire exceeds the amount that is freely available.

scarcity—The result of an inability to satisfy all of everyone's wants. Supplies of the factors of production are limited.

scenario analysis—Testing plans against possible scenarios to see what might happen should things not go as hoped.

SDR—Special drawing rights. Created in 1967, the SDR is the IMF's own currency. Its value is based on a portfolio of widely used currencies. The SDR was created in 1969 to supplement a shortfall of preferred foreign exchange reserve assets, namely gold and the U.S. dollar.

seasonal unemployment—Unemployment caused by seasonal shifts in labor supply and demand. Example: ski instructors are unemployed in summer.

seasonally adjusted—There are seasonal patterns in many economic activities. For instance, there is less construction in winter than in summer, and spending in shops soars as Christmas approaches. To reveal underlying trends, statistics reflecting only part of the year are often adjusted to iron out seasonal variations.

second-best criticism—If the economy is not currently at the competitive equilibrium, it is not at all clear that particular moves toward a competitive equilibrium will be in society's best interest. (See *normative criticism*.)

secondary effects—Unintended consequences of economic actions that develop slowly over time as people react to events. Example: Government imposes rent controls on housing, so owners abandon their buildings because they lack sufficient funds to maintain their properties.

secondary financial market—A market in which previously owned securities are bought and sold. Stock markets such as the New York Stock Exchange are secondary markets.

security—A certificate that represents either ownership interest in a business (for example, a share of stock) or an obligation of indebtedness owed by an institution (for example, a bond). Also known as financial instrument.

Securities and Exchange Commission—In the United States government, an independent, nonpartisan, quasi-judicial regulatory agency with responsibility for administering the federal securities laws.

securities laws—Legislation and regulations intended to protect investors and to ensure that they have access to disclosure of all relevant information concerning publicly traded securities.

securities markets—Places or systems in which stocks, bonds, and other financial instruments are bought and sold.

seigniorage—The difference between the face value of money and the cost of supplying it; the "profit" from issuing money. Example: The government pays five cents to produce a one-dollar bill; the seigniorage is 95 cents.

seller's market—A market in which the seller seems to have the upper hand and so can charge a higher price than in a buyer's market.

seniority—The importance assigned to a worker's length of service when it comes to such matters as promotions, pay raises, layoffs, vacation, and sick leave.

services—Economic activities that normally are consumed as they are produced, as contrasted with goods, which are more tangible. These may include, among others, such activities as transportation, banking, insurance, tourism, telecommunications, advertising, entertainment, data processing, and consulting.

Sherman Antitrust Act—Law passed by U.S. Congress in 1890 to attempt to regulate the competitive process. A landmark federal statute in the history of United States antitrust law (or "competition law"). It prohibits certain business activities that federal government regulators deem to be anti-competitive, and requires the federal government to investigate and pursue *trusts*.

shift factors of demand—Something other than price that affects how much of a good is demanded. (Contrast with *movement along a demand curve*.)

shift in demand—A shift of the entire demand curve.

shift in supply—A shift of the entire supply curve.

shock—An unexpected event that affects an economy

short run—Period of time in which a producer has at least one fixed resource. (Contrast with *long run*.)

short-run aggregate supply (SRAS) curve—A curve that shows the direct relation between the price level and the quantity of aggregate output supplied, other things remaining constant.

short-run decision—The firm is constrained in regard to what production decisions it can make. (Contrast with *long-run decision.*)

short-run Phillips curve—A curve that, based on an expected price level, purports to reflect an inverse relation between the inflation rate and the level of unemployment.

short-term assets—Assets that a company expects to readily convert into cash or consume within the current accounting period, typically one year. (Contrast with *long-term assets.*)

short-termism—Doing things that make you better off in the short-run but worse off in the end.

shortage—An unstable market situation that occurs when quantity demanded exceeds quantity supplied. (Contrast with *surplus.*)

shorting—Selling a security, such as a share, that you do not currently own, in the expectation that its price will fall by the time the security has to be delivered to its new owner. If the price does fall, you can buy the security at the lower price, deliver it to whomever you sold it and make a profit. The risk is that the price rises, leaving you with a loss.

shutdown point—Point at which the firm will gain more by shutting down than it will by staying in business.

shutdown rule—Any firm in the short run should shut down if its price is less than its average variable costs.

SIC—See *Standard Industrial Code.*

simple interest—The type of interest that is earned on the original principal only. Contrast with compound interest.

simple money multiplier—The reciprocal of the required reserve ratio, or $1/r$.

sin tax—Tax designed to discourage activities society believes are harmful to individuals. Example: Governments impose high taxes on cigarettes, which are known to cause cancer, heart disease, and other catastrophic illnesses.

size distribution of income—The relative division or allocation of total income among income groups.

Smith, Adam—Scottish social philosopher and pioneer of political economy, author of *An Inquiry into the Nature and Causes of the Wealth of Nations*, considered his magnum opus and the first modern work of economics. It earned him an reputation and would become one of the most influential works on economics ever published. Smith is widely cited as the father of modern economics and capitalism.

Adam Smith (1723-1790)

social benefits/costs—The overall impact of an economic activity on the welfare of society. Social benefits/costs are the sum of private benefits/costs arising from the activity and any externalities.

social capital—The amount of community spirit or trust that an economy has gluing it together. In general, the more social capital there is, the more productive the economy will be.

social efficiency rule—Any activity should be undertaken in an amount at which its marginal benefit equals its marginal cost. (In production of a good, this means where P = MC.)

social science—A subject that through research tries to explain why society acts the way it does and tries to form theories to predict what may happen in the future.

social regulation— Refers to the broad category of rules governing how any business or individual carries out its activities, with a view to correcting one or more "market failures." A classic way in which the market fails is when firms (or individuals) do not take account the costs their activities may impose on third parties (see *externalities*). When this happens, the activities will be pursued too intensely or in ways that fail to stem harm to third parties. For example, left to its own devices, a manufacturing plant may spew harmful chemicals into the air and water, causing harm to its neighbors. Governments respond to this problem by setting standards for emissions or even by requiring that firms use specific technologies, such as "scrubbers" for utilities that capture noxious chemicals before steam is released into the air).

Social Security—A U.S. government pension program that provides financial benefits to retirees based on their own and their employers' contributions to the program while they were working. Also provides financial benefits to the disabled and to other eligible dependents and survivors.

socialism—An economic system in which the basic means of production are primarily owned and controlled collectively, usually by government under some system of central planning. Equity is emphasized at the expense of efficiency.

socioeconomic distribution of income—The relative division or allocation of total income among relevant socioeconomic groups.

sole proprietorship—A business owned by one person.

Solow–Swan model—An exogenous growth model, a model of long-run economic growth set within the framework of neoclassical economics. It attempts to explain long-run economic growth by looking at capital accumulation, labor or population growth, and increases in productivity, commonly referred to as technological progress. The model was developed independently by Robert Solow and Trevor Swan in 1956.

sovereign risk—The risk that a government will default on its debt or on a loan guaranteed by it.

sow's ear effect—The inability of a country to raise its productivity or per capita GDP relative to other countries of similar development despite policy adjustments in macroeconomic variables (e.g., the exchange rate or rate of interest) because of deficiencies on the supply side of the economy, (e.g., an inadequately educated labor force). The term refers to the old saying "You can't make a silk purse out of a sow's ear."

Special Drawing Rights—See *SDR*.

specialization—Production of a limited variety of products by a business, region, or nation.

speculator—A person who buys or sells foreign exchange in hopes of profiting from fluctuations in the exchange rate over time.

spot price—The price quoted for a transaction to be made on the spot, i.e., paid for now for delivery now. Contrast spot markets with forward contracts and futures markets, where payment and delivery will be made at a future date.

stabilization—Government policies intended to smooth the economic cycle, expanding demand when unemployment is high and reducing it when inflation threatens to increase.

stagflation—An economic condition of both continuing inflation and stagnant business activity characterized by high unemployment.

stagnation—A prolonged recession, not as severe as depression.

stakeholders—All the parties who have an interest, financial or otherwise, in a company, including shareholders, creditors, bondholders, employees, customers, management, the community, and government. How these different interests should be catered for, and what to do when they conflict, is much debated. In particular, there is growing disagreement between those who argue that companies should be run primarily in the interests of their shareholders, in order to maximize shareholder value, and those who argue that the wishes of shareholders should sometimes be traded off against those of other stakeholders.

Standard Industrial Code—System for classifying industries. The more digits in the code, the more detail there is in the classification. A 2-digit industry is a broadly defined industrial group; a 4-digit industry is a more specific type of industry within the more broadly defined 2-digit group.

standard of living—A minimum of necessities, comforts, or luxuries considered essential to maintaining a person or group in customary or proper status or circumstances.

standard of value—A common unit for measuring the value of every good or service.

state socialism—Economic system in which government sees to it that people work for the common good rather than relying on people to do that on their own. Directly conflicts with Adam Smith's "invisible hand" theory.

statement of cash flow—A financial statement that provides information about the company's cash receipts, cash disbursements, and net change in cash during a specified period.

statistically significant—The probability of getting a particular result by chance is low. The most commonly used measure of statistical significance is that there must be a 95 percent chance that the result is right and only a 1 in 20 chance of the result occurring randomly.

sterilized intervention—When a government or central bank buys or sells some of its reserves of foreign currency, this can affect the country's money supply. Selling reserves decreases the supply of the domestic currency; buying reserves increases the domestic money supply. Governments or central banks can sterilize (that is, cancel out) this effect of foreign exchange intervention on the money supply by buying or selling an equivalent amount of securities. For example, if the government increases reserves by buying foreign currency the domestic money supply will increase, unless it sells securities such as treasury bills to mop up the extra demand.

stochastic process—A process that exhibits random behavior. For instance, Brownian motion (from botanist Robert Brown), which is often used to describe changes in share prices in an efficient market (the random walk), is a stochastic process.

stock—Ownership shares in the assets of a corporation. Also, a variable that measures the amount of something at a particular point in time, such as the amount of money you have right now.

stock exchange—An organized financial market for the buying and selling of stocks and bonds.

stockholder—A person or organization who owns stock in a company and, thus, partially owns that company. Also known as shareholder.

store of wealth—Anything that retains its purchasing power over time.

strategic behavior—When a firm manager makes decisions based in part on the anticipated reactions of the firm's rivals.

stress-testing—A process for exploring how a portfolio of assets and/or liabilities would fare in extreme adverse conditions. A useful tool in risk management.

strike—Work stoppage to force management to accept union demands.

structural adjustment—A program of policies designed to change the structure of an economy. Usually, the term refers to adjustment towards a market economy, under a program approved by the IMF or World Bank, which often supply structural adjustment funds to ease the pain of transition. Such policies are much criticized in the developing world, sometimes with good reason.

structural unemployment—Unemployment caused by changes in technology, consumer preference, or movement of jobs from one location to another. These changes result in obsolete job skills with job-seekers whose skills do not match those needed for any reasonably available job.

subjective—Allowing one's personal views or value judgments to affect one's analysis. (Contrast with *objective*.)

subprime mortgage—A type of loan granted to individuals with poor credit histories who would not be able to qualify for conventional mortgages. With a higher risk for lenders, subprime mortgages charge interest rates well above the prime lending rate. Subprime mortgages failed in great numbers, contributing to the near collapse of the financial system and deep recession in 2008.

subsidiary—A company that is owned and controlled by another company but operates separately from the parent company.

subsidy—An economic benefit, direct or indirect, granted by a government to domestic producers of specified goods or services, often to strengthen their competitive position against more efficient foreign suppliers. For example, in some states of the United States, companies producing liquid biofuels receive direct subsidies for every gallon of ethanol they produce. Subsidies are generally prohibited by the World Trade Organization agreement.

subsistence wage theory—The idea that capitalists will maximize profits by paying workers only the bare minimum required for them to survive. Contrast with efficiency wage theory.

substitutes—Two or more goods that serve roughly the same purpose to buyers. Corn and wheat are substitutes for producing breakfast cereals. (Contrast with *complements*.)

substitution effect—When the price of a good falls, consumers will substitute it for other goods, which remain relatively more expensive.

sunk cost—A cost that cannot be recovered and that is therefore irrelevant when an economic choice is being made.

supply—Quantities that will be brought to market at various prices. The total quantity of goods and services producers are willing and able to sell at all possible prices during some time period. (Contrast with *demand*.)

supply curve—A graph of the relationship between the price of a good and the amount supplied at different prices. (See also *demand curve*.)

supply shocks—Unexpected events that affect aggregate supply; sometimes the effect is only temporary. Example: OPEC nations suddenly reduced oil exports to the U.S. and other nations in the 1970s, sharply raising prices.

supply-side economics—Macroeconomic policy that focuses on the use of tax cuts to stimulate production so as to increase aggregate supply. Typically supported by wealthy individuals and by businesses. (See *trickle-down theory*.)

supply-side fiscal policy—Intended to increase an economy's productive capacity by shifting aggregate supply; e.g., a tax cut giving businesses an incentive to invest and expand.

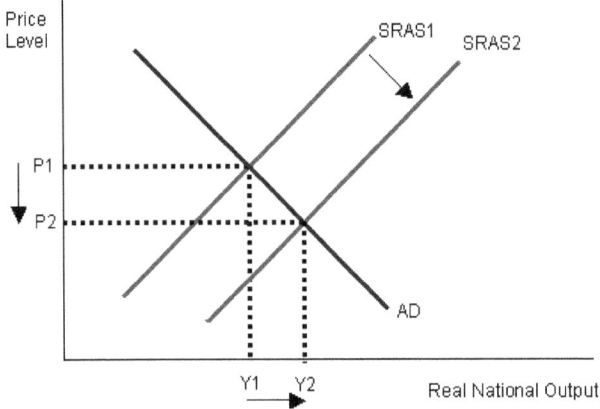

Aggregate supply shifts to the right, stimulating real growth and lowering price level.

surplus—An unstable market situation that occurs when quantity supplied exceeds quantity demanded.

systematic risk—The risk that remains after diversification, also known as market risk or undiversifiable risk. It is systematic risk that determines the return earned on a well-diversified portfolio of assets.

systemic risk—The risk of damage being done to the health of the financial system as a whole.

T-account—A diagram used to illustrate changes in the assets and liabilities of a bank's balance sheet. A T-account, so named because of its perpendicular lines that look like a T, represents changes in assets on the left and changes in liabilities and net worth on the right.

Taft-Hartley Act—A Congressional act passed in 1947 that limited the power acquired by U.S. labor unions during the 1930s and into the 1940s. Officially known as the Labor-Management Relations Act, this outlawed unfair labor practices by labor unions to counterbalance earlier legislation that had outlawed unfair labor practices by firms. The Taft-Hartley Act also set up provisions to decertify unions if members chose to do so, and allowed states to pass what are euphemistically called "right-to-work laws," which would outlaw union shops.

takeover—Purchase of a firm by another firm that then takes direct control over its operations. (See *merger, acquisition,* and *hostile takeover.*)

tangible assets—Assets you can touch, e.g., buildings, machinery, gold, works of art. Contrast with intangible assets.

target market—A group of consumers to whom a business will attempt to sell a particular product.

tariff—A tax imposed on goods imported from one customs area to another either for protective or revenue purposes.

tax—A payment to government.

tax avoidance—Doing everything possible within the law to reduce your tax bill. Learned Hand, an American judge, once said: "There is nothing sinister in so arranging one's affairs as to keep taxes as low as possible ... nobody owes any public duty to pay more than the law demands." Contrast with *tax evasion.*

tax base—The thing or amount to which a tax rate applies.

tax burden—Total tax paid in a period as a proportion of total income in that period. It can refer to personal, corporate, or national income.

tax evasion—The crime of paying less tax than you are legally obliged to. Contrast with *tax avoidance*. There may be a thin line between the two, but as Denis Healey, a former British chancellor, once put it, "The difference between tax avoidance and tax evasion is the thickness of a prison wall."

tax haven—A country or designated zone that has low or no taxes, or highly secretive banks, and often a warm climate and sandy beaches, which make it attractive to foreigners bent on tax avoidance or even tax evasion.

tax incentive program—Any program in which a tax is used to create incentives for individuals to structure their activities in a way that is consistent with particular desired outcomes.

tax incidence—The final impact of a tax; who will really have to pay the tax.

tax proportionality—The proportion of income paid in taxes at different levels of income. In some taxes the proportion of income paid in taxes increases with income (progressive); in other cases it decreases (regressive). In still other cases, it remains the same (flat).

tax rate—The percentage at which an individual or corporation is taxed. The tax rate is imposed by the federal government and some states based on an individual's taxable income or a corporation's earnings.

tax withholding—A deduction for income taxes that is taken from a disbursement and sent to a federal, state, or provincial tax authority and that reduces the amount of income taxes that must later be submitted.

team spirit—The feelings of friendship and being part of a team that bring out people's best effort.

technical efficiency—A situation in which as few inputs as possible are used to produce a given output. (See *economically efficient*.)

technical progress—A crucial ingredient of economic growth. Economists used to take a certain rate of technological progress for granted. In *endogenous growth theory*, they make more effort to measure accurately and better understand what causes differences in the rate of technical change.

technological change—An increase in the range of production techniques that provides new ways of producing goods.

technology shocks—Events in a macroeconomic model that change the production function. Usually this is modeled with an aggregate production function that has a scaling factor. It may be a positive shock, increasing the output for a given set of inputs, or a negative shock, decreasing the output for a given set of inputs. Negative shocks are much less common than positive shocks as technology rarely moves backwards.

telemarketing—A direct response sales method that uses the telephone to produce sales. Very often perceived as a nuisance by consumers.

terms of trade—An indication of how much of one good will be exchanged for a unit of another good.

Third way—An economic philosophy espoused by some leftish political leaders in the late 20th century, including Bill Clinton and Tony Blair. According to the rhetoric, it is not capitalism and not socialism, but a third (pragmatic) way. Many have therefore found it rather hard to pin down. It was earlier used to describe Sweden's economic model.

thrifts—Savings and loan organizations, mutual savings banks, credit unions.

tick—The minimum price change possible in a financial marketplace.

time deposits—Deposits that earn a fixed rate of interest if held for a specified period, which can range anywhere from 30 days to several years.

time inconsistency problem—The problem that arises when policy makers have an incentive to announce one policy to influence expectations but then pursue a different policy once those expectations have been formed and acted upon.

time series—Several measurements of a variable taken at regular intervals, such as daily, monthly, quarterly, and so on. They are often used by economists in search of trends that they hope will let them predict future movements in the variable.

time value of money—The idea that a dollar today is worth more than a dollar in the future, because the dollar in the hand today can earn interest during the time until the future dollar is received.

Tobin's Q—A financial measure of a firm's returns, calculated by dividing the market value of the firm (the market value of its outstanding stock and debt) by the replacement costs of the firm's assets. According to James Tobin of Yale University, Nobel Laureate in Economics in 1981, if this ratio is greater than 1 it means the firm is earning a rate of return higher than that justified by the costs of its assets. Tobin suggested the ratio of the market value of a firm to the replacement costs of its assets should be close to 1.

token money—Money whose face value exceeds value from which it is made, e.g., coins and paper bills.

total cost—The sum of total fixed cost + total variable cost. $TC = ATC \times Q$, where TC is total cost, ATC is average total cost, and Q is quantity produced.

total fixed costs—The sum of a firm's short run costs that do not increase as a firm's total product increases.

total product (total output, Q)—Total number of units of a product that a firm has produced.

total profit (Π)—Total revenue minus total costs.

$$\Pi = (P \times Q) - (ATC \times Q)$$

total quality management (TQM)—A management theory of the late 20th century to improve productivity and product quality.

total return—The sum of all the different benefits from investing in an ASSET, including INCOME paid to the investor and any change in the market value of the asset. The total return is often expressed as a percentage of the amount invested.

total revenue—Total dollar value of a firm's sales.

Total revenue = P x Q

total utility—Total satisfaction one gets from one's entire consumption of a product. (Contrast with *marginal utility*.)

total variable costs—The sum of a firm's costs that increase as its total product increases.

trade adjustment assistance programs—Programs designed to compensate those who suffer losses when trade restrictions are reduced.

trade barrier—A measure designed to slow or prevent trading between nations.

trade deficit—The amount of money by which a country's merchandise imports exceed its merchandise exports.

trademark—A unique design, name, or symbol that identifies a product, service, or company, usually registered and protected by law.

trade-off—A choice that involves giving up some of one thing to have more of another. "There ain't no such thing as a free lunch!"

trade surplus—The amount of money by which a country's merchandise exports exceed its merchandise imports.

trade-weighted exchange rate—A country's exchange rate with the currencies of its trading partners weighted by the amount of trade done by the country in each currency.

traditional economy—A system in which the basic economic questions of what to produce, how to produce it, and who should get what is produced are generally answered by traditions and customs.

transaction costs—The costs incurred during the process of buying or selling, on top of the price of whatever is changing hands. If these costs can be reduced, the price mechanism will operate more efficiently.

transactions demand for money—Money demanded as a medium of exchange.

transfer payments—Payments that are made without any good or service being received in return. Much public spending goes on transfers, such as pensions and welfare benefits. Private-sector transfers include charitable donations and prizes to lottery winners.

transfer pricing—Prices assumed, for the purposes of calculating tax liability, charged by one unit of a multinational company when selling to another (foreign) unit of the same firm to minimize their total tax bill. By charging low transfer prices from a unit based in a high-tax country that is selling to a unit in a low-tax country, a firm can record a low profit in the first country and a high profit in the second.

transitional nations' economies—The economic transition of eastern and central European countries is a multi-phase process of abandoning communist economic institutions and mechanisms and replacing them with market structures and dynamics.

travelers' checks—Prepaid checks sold by banks and other firms that may be replaced if lost or stolen.

treasury bills (T-bills)—A type of low risk security issued and guaranteed by the U.S. government that can easily be converted into cash. Issued for terms of less than a year. Purchasers are lending money to the government.

treasury stock—Stock that has been repurchased at market price
   by the issuing company with the intention of reselling the
   stock at a later date.

trend—A change that occurs over time.

Long-term growth linear trend of U.S. Real GDP

trend analysis—A type of financial analysis that involves
   calculating percentage changes in financial statement items
   over several successive accounting periods, rather than over
   just two periods.

trickle-down theory—The widely discredited belief that giving
   benefits to the rich will expand aggregate output and
   thereby help the poor. Also called *Reaganomics.*

trough—The lowest point in the business cycle.

tying—A sales practice prohibited in the U.S. in which a firm
   makes the completion of one transaction, such as approval
   for a loan, dependent upon another transaction, such as the
   purchase of insurance.

U

underemployment—A situation in which workers are overqualified for their jobs or work fewer hours than they would prefer.

underground economy—Exchanges of goods and services not reported to the government for tax purposes.

unemployed (officially)—In the U.S., to be officially unemployed, one must not be working at all for pay, be actively seeking work, and be 16 years of age or older.

unemployment—The number of people of working age without a job who are looking for work.

unemployment compensation—Short-term financial assistance, regardless of need, to eligible individuals who are temporarily out of work.

unemployment rate—The number of people officially unemployed (over 16, willing and able to work, seeking jobs) divided by the number of people in the labor force.

Unfair Trade Practices Act—A law that many U.S. states have enacted that defines certain business acts as unfair and prohibits those practices in business.

union shop—Requires workers to join a union once they are hired, or to pay a portion of the union dues that may be fairly attributed to the value of the union to the worker, e.g., in collective bargaining agreements. (Contrast with *closed shop* and *open shop*.)

unit cost—The cost of producing one item, determined by dividing total costs by the number produced.

unit elastic—An elasticity alternative in which any percentage change in price causes an equal percentage change in quantity: ($E_d = 1$). In other words, any change in price, whether big or small, triggers exactly the same percentage change in quantity. Unit elastic should be compared with other elasticity alternatives—perfectly elastic, perfectly inelastic, relatively elastic, and relatively inelastic.

U.S. Government securities—Treasury notes, treasury bills, treasury bonds, issued by the U.S. Treasury to finance budget deficits.

usury—Charging an exorbitant rate of interest.

util—A theoretical numerical measure of utility.

utilitarian—Philosophy of equity stating that society should maximize the sum of citizens' utilities.

utility—The pleasure or satisfaction one gets from consuming a good or service. (Contrast with *total utility* and *marginal utility*.)

utility-maximizing rule—A household should purchase units of items that provide it with the highest marginal utility per dollar, so when its spendable income is exhausted the marginal utility per dollar for all goods consumed is equal.

utopian socialism—Ideal state where social and economic arrangements appeal to people's higher nature.

utopians—People who believe that a society of abundance without conflict is possible, that good results come from good motives and good motives lead to good results.

❧ V ❧

value—Amount of consumer satisfaction obtained from a good, service, or resource. The more a good satisfies a person's want or need, the more valuable it is to that person. Different people are likely to place different values on a good. Resources are valuable to the degree that they are used to produce things that consumers want.

value added—Contribution made to the final value of a good at each stage of production. Defined as the value of the firm's output minus the value of all its inputs purchased from other firms.

value-added tax (VAT)—Tax levied on the value added to goods at every stage of production.

value of marginal product—Marginal physical product times the price that the firm can sell that product for.

variable costs—Costs that vary with the amount of business a firm does. Fixed costs plus variable costs equals total costs.

variable interest rate—An interest rate that fluctuates according to the rise and fall of interest rates in the marketplace.

velocity of money—The average number of times a year a unit of national currency is used to purchase final goods and services.

venture capital—Investment in a new, generally high-risk, enterprise.

vertical merger—A combination of two companies, one being a buyer of the products the other company sells. (Contrast with *horizontal merger*.)

volatility—The most widely accepted measure of risk in financial markets is the amount by which the price of a security swings up and down. The more volatile the price, the riskier is the security.

voluntary exchange—The process of trading that occurs in markets.

❧ W ❧

wage drift—The difference between basic pay and total earnings. Wage drift consists of things such as overtime payments, bonuses, profit share and performance-related pay. It usually increases during periods of strong growth and declines during an economic downturn.

wages—Earnings of workers paid on an hourly basis. Also used for all payments to employees.

Wall Street—A street in lower Manhattan, New York City, center of the Financial District. Home to the New York Stock Exchange.

warranty—A promise or guarantee that a statement of fact is true. The statement is made by a party to a contract at the time of contracting, becomes a part of the contract, and if not literally true, gives the other party a ground to rescind the contract.

wealth—The value of assets an individual owns.

wealth effect—As people get wealthier, they consume more. This wealth effect has important consequences for monetary policy. When there is an interest rate increase, future income from assets such as equities must be discounted at a higher rate than before. As a result their owners feel poorer and spend less. A cut in interest rates has the opposite effect.

Wealth of Nations—Short title of a book published by Scottish philosopher and economist Adam Smith in 1776: *An Enquiry into the Nature and Causes of the Wealth of Nations.* Smith asks, "Why is it that some nations grow rich while others remain poor?" By reflecting upon the economics at the beginning of the Industrial Revolution, the book touches upon such broad topics as the division of labor, productivity, and free markets.

wealth tax—Also called a capital tax, equity tax, or net worth tax, a levy on the total value of personal assets, including owner-occupied housing; cash, bank deposits, money funds, and savings in insurance and pension plans; investment in real estate and unincorporated businesses; and corporate stock, financial securities, and personal trusts. Typically liabilities (primarily mortgages and other loans) are deducted, hence it is sometimes called a net wealth tax.

Weightless economy—At the start of the 21st century, the total output of the American economy weighed roughly the same as it did 100 years earlier. Yet the value of that output, in real terms, was 20 times greater. Output is increasingly weightless, produced from intellectual capital rather than physical materials. Production has shifted from steel, heavy copper wire and vacuum tubes to microprocessors, fine fiber-optic cables and transistors. services have increased their share of GDP. This weightless or dematerialized economy, most economists agree, is not just lighter but also more efficient.

welfare—Enjoyment of necessary resources for a worthwhile life. Americans use welfare as shorthand for government handouts to the poor. Economists use it to describe the wellbeing of an individual or society, as in "Are tax cuts welfare-enhancing?" This is economist-speak for "Will tax cuts improve the overall wellbeing of the country?"

welfare capitalism—Economic system in which the market operates but government regulates markets significantly.

welfare economics—That part of economics concerned with the effects of economic activity on welfare, *viz.*, enjoyment of the necessary resources for a worthwhile life. The study of how different forms of economic activity and different methods of allocating scarce resources affect the wellbeing of different individuals or countries.

welfare loss triangle—Representation of the welfare cost in terms of the resource misallocation caused by monopoly.

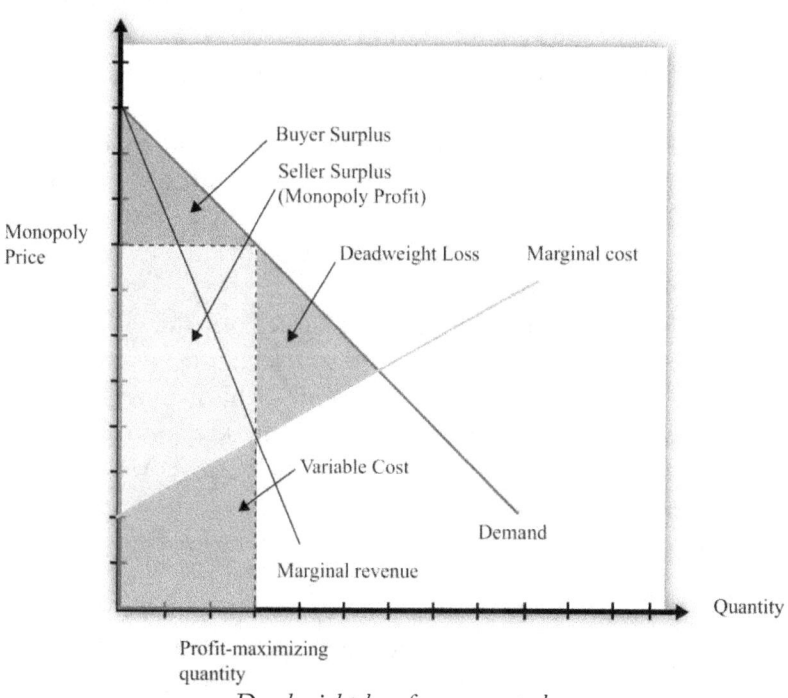

Deadweight loss from monopoly

World Bank—International Bank for Reconstruction and
    Development. Along with the International Monetary
    Fund, founded at an international conference at Bretton
    Woods, New Hampshire, in 1944.
World Trade Organization (WTO)—An international treaty and
    structure, successor to the General Agreement on Tariffs
    and Trade (GATT), set up during the Uruguay Round of
    GATT in 1994, that aims to reduce trade barriers around
    the world. Most nations of the world are signatories to the
    WTO and have agreed to abide by its rules and decisions.

X—The standard abbreviation for exports produced by the foreign sector and purchased by the domestic economy, especially when used in the study of macroeconomics. This abbreviation is most often seen in the aggregate expenditure equation, $GDP = C + I + G + (X - M)$, where C, I, G, and $(X - M)$ represent expenditures by the four macroeconomic sectors, household, business, government, and foreign. The United States, for example, sells many products produced within its boundaries to other countries, including wheat, beef, cars, furniture, and others.

X-inefficiency—Operating a firm far less efficiently than it could be operated technically. Cost is higher than it needs to be because a firm is operating inefficiently. This is most often seen for firms that have a great deal of market control, especially monopoly. The lack of competition allows a business to pad its expenses, hire unneeded employees (like relatives), goof off instead of working, and all sorts of other things that lessen production and increase cost. The business is not penalized for these actions, because market control allows the company to extract whatever price is needed to cover cost, subject to market demand.

X-M—Net exports, the difference between exports, goods and services produced by the domestic economy and purchased by the foreign sector, and imports, goods and services produced by the foreign sector and purchased by the domestic economy. While exports and imports are important unto themselves, when combined into a single measure net exports captures the overall interaction between the foreign sector and the domestic economy. If exports exceed imports, then net exports are positive, and if imports exceed exports, the net exports are negative.

❧ Y ❧

Y-axis—In a graph, one of two lines that intersect at a right angle. This is the "vertical axis" that runs up and down.

yankee bond—A bond issued with a dollar denomination in the United States by a foreign bank or corporation. This allows U.S. investors to invest in foreign securities without price fluctuations caused by volatile exchange rates.

yellow-dog contract—An agreement signed by workers before they are hired in which they promise not to join a union; outlawed in the United States in 1935 by the Norris-LaGuardia Act. This contract was commonly used by firms in the late 1800s and early 1900s to limit labor union membership and thus prevent unions from influencing the labor market.

yield—Actual amount of interest earned; depends on the rate of return and the frequency of compounding.

yield curve—A curve plotting the yields (or returns) on securities with different maturity lengths. The standard yield is for U.S. Treasury securities with lengths ranging from 90 days to 30 years. The six maturity lengths are usually 90 day, 180 day, 2 year, 5 year, 10 year, and 30 year. The shape and slope of the yield curve indicates the state of the economy and what's likely to come. A normal yield curve has a slight positive slope, with slightly higher yields for longer maturity securities. A steep yield curve suggests the end of a contraction and beginning of an expansion. An inverted, or negatively sloped yield curve is the sign of an upcoming contraction.

YTM—Yield to maturity, the annual rate of return on a financial asset that is held until maturity. Yield to maturity depends on both the coupon rate and the face or par value paid at maturity.

❧ Z ☙

zero-based budgeting (ZBB)—A budgeting process in which a company begins with the premise that no resources will be allocated for the next accounting period unless and until each expense is shown to be in accord with the company's strategic and operational goals.

zero-coupon bond—A certificate reflecting the promise of a firm or government to pay the holder a fixed sum of money on the designated maturing date. These bonds pay no interest but are sold at a discount from their face value. Buyers of these bonds hope to sell later at or above the face value.

zero growth—A growth rate (usually in terms of population) that is equal to zero. In other words, there is no change from one year to the next. This goal has been proposed by those who contend that population growth is placing excessive pressure on the planet's availability of limited resources and its ability to assimilate pollution. In general terms, zero growth can apply to any measurement, including production, prices, etc.

zero profit condition—Requirement that in the long-run competitive equilibrium, there are zero economic profits.

zero slope—A horizontal line in which the numerical value of the slope, calculated as the change in the variable on the vertical axis divided by a change in the variable on the horizontal axis, is zero. In other words, the Y-axis variable is fixed, or constant, for any and all values of the X-axis variable.

zero-sum game—A situation in which a fixed amount is divided up among the winners and losers. In a zero-sum game the wins equal the losses.

zoning—Legal restrictions on where different activities can locate within a city. Most cities regulate the location of industrial, commercial, and residential activities.

References

AmosWEB: http://www.amosweb.com.
Bade, R., & Parkin, M. (2015). *Foundations of macroeconomics*. Boston: Pearson.
Bannock, G., Baxter, R. E., & Davis E. (1998). *The Penguin dictionary of economics*. London: Penguin.
Black, J. (1997). *Oxford dictionary of economics*. Oxford: Oxford University Press.
Blanchard, O., & Johnson, D. R. (2013). *Macroeconomics, 6th ed*. Upper Saddle River, NJ: Pearson.
Central Intelligence Agency. (2016). *World factbook*. Washington: CIA.
Colander, D. C. (2013). *Microeconomics, 9th ed*. New York: Irwin.
Econguru. (2016). http://glossary.econguru.com/
Economist. (2016). http://www.economist.com/economics-a-to-z
Farlex. (2016). *Financial dictionary*. (2012). Retrieved June 30, 2016 from http://financial-dictionary.thefreedictionary.com.
Junior Achievement (2000). *JA economics*. Colorado Springs, CO: JA.
King, W. http://william-king.www.drexel.edu/.
Mankiw, G. N. (2015). *Principles of economics, 7th ed*. South-Western.
Melberg, H. O. (2016). *Definitions of economics: A short and uncritical introduction. http://www.oocities.org/hmelberg/papers/981123.htm*
Mish, F. C. (Ed.). (1993). *Merriam-Webster's collegiate dictionary*, 10th ed. Springfield, Massachusetts: Merriam-Webster.
Warner, M. (1997). *The IEBM pocket encyclopedia of business and management*. New York: Thomson Business Press.
Wikipedia. Various pages and years

The Editors gratefully acknowledge the many sources of images and definitions from the Internet in addition to those noted above.